THE LITTLE BOOK
OF
PICKING TOP
STOCKS

THE LITTLE BOOK

OF
PICKING TOP
STOCKS

How to Spot the Hidden Gems

Martin S. Fridson

WILEY

Published by John Wiley & Sons, Inc., Hoboken, New Jersey.
Published simultaneously in Canada.

For general information on our other products and services or for technical support, please contact our Customer Care Department within the United States at (800) 762-2974, outside the United States at (317) 572-3993 or fax (317) 572-4002.

Wiley also publishes its books in a variety of electronic formats. Some content that appears in print may not be available in electronic formats. For more information about Wiley products, visit our web site at www.wiley.com.

Library of Congress Cataloging-in-Publication Data is Available:

ISBN 9781394176618 (Hardback)
ISBN 9781394176069 (ePDF)
ISBN 9781394176045 (epub)

Cover Design and Image: Wiley

SKY10041150_030923

*This book is dedicated to my brother Howard Fridson,
who has set an outstanding example by helping friends
and loved ones through life's challenges.*

Contents

Foreword

MARTY FRIDSON IS A Renaissance man, a rarity on Wall Street.

He's a brilliant investor, a historian (of more than just capital markets), and a music aficionado. He has a wit that's wicked, especially for wordplay. He's also a source of inspiration to many, particularly me.

Our careers overlap almost to the day; our trajectories diverged almost immediately; but over the decades, we've had a few memorable points of intersection. I started at Drexel Burnham; Marty at Mitchell Hutchins. I took the equity path; Marty focused on fixed income. I soon went entrepreneurial; Marty made an impressive set of rounds at a number of top-flight firms. I was once dubbed "Wall Street's

Clipping Service"; Marty became "the Dean of the High-Yield Market." We became friends decades ago through our work at the CFA Institute (née AIMR).

From the CFA Institute to the *Financial Analysts Journal*, Marty's contributions to the investment profession are significant. Many authors live in fear of Marty in his role as a reviewer on the *Enterprising Investor* blog. They live in particular fear of his last paragraph because it usually reveals the errors he's discovered in their work—facts, language, historical context . . . yikes! They don't complain; they know that, as an author/editor himself of a dozen important titles, he's earned the right to critique. (It's impressive that the likes of Peter Bernstein and Jack Bogle thanked him for his corrections!)

When Marty writes, he brings his Renaissance self to his work regardless of the topic. His investment thesis is always accompanied by a rich lesson in market history. As an added benefit to the reader, he can never resist layering in an orchestra of musical references based on his innate love of music and the immersion his wife, Elaine Sisman, provides as professor of music at Columbia.

Ultimately, Marty writes as an investor. As chief investment officer of Lehmann Livian Fridson Advisors, he describes his investment approach as "quantamental." For the uninitiated, a quantamentalist is the Holy Grail of

Wall Street—someone who knows numbers and combines them with fundamental analysis. In what he delivers to his reader, Marty goes well beyond the numbers. He combines the insights of a seasoned security analyst with the computational precision of a fixed-income investor. The best illustration of his brilliant alchemy, in its fifth edition, is *Financial Statement Analysis: A Practitioner's Guide.*

The latest tour de force of the dean of the high-yield market is a title that might surprise—*The Little Book of Picking Top Stocks.* In fact, a high-yield bond investor like Marty has the strength of experience in fundamentals and number-crunching to offer important qualitative and quantitative insights. Although the title may remind you of other investment books you've read, like Marty it is one of a kind—insightful, informative, and provocative—with the added advantage of being right!

The path of my investment career is better for the times it crossed with Marty's. As an investor and a lifelong student of the market, I'm better off for the richness of his writing. In *The Little Book of Picking Top Stocks*, the polymath Martin Fridson shares the wealth with all of us.

Theodore R. Aronson

Co-founder, AJO Vista

Former chairman, CFA Institute

Preface

$\sim$

Brace yourself. You're about to see the stock market from a radically new angle. The focus of this book is figuring out which stock is going to be the year's single best performer in the S&P 500 Index. In the period studied here, those stocks have produced one-year total returns ranging from 80% to 743%.

You've read the standard investment approach lots of times. Financial institutions and personal wealth advisors present familiar themes: "Focus on the long term. Diversify. Stick to high-quality companies with dependable earnings and proven management." These are wise words, well worth heeding if you hope for a secure financial future.

But let's face it. Those prudent principles don't even vaguely describe the actions of certain investors. A non-trivial percentage of people who buy stocks are shooting for a monster payday. Not between now and retirement in 40 years but immediately. Or sooner. They have zero interest in "hitting a lot of singles." They're swinging for a grand slam, game over, right this very inning.

The instant gratification style of investing made headlines on the business page and beyond in 2021. Hordes of market newcomers became obsessed with meme stocks. The shares of a few companies with a ton of social media buzz went to the moon—and back, in some cases.

Meme fans weren't thinking about funding their retirement or their yet unborn kids' college education. Fundamental analysis played no part in their "stonk"-picking. Some of these plungers even boasted that they knew absolutely nothing about the companies they were throwing money at. Nor did they care one iota about spreading risk. One influencer advised: When you decide on a YOLO (you only live once) trade, put 98% to 100% of your portfolio in it.[1]

Aiming for one colossal win isn't a new idea. In every market boom of the past few centuries, sudden and spectacular wealth creation dazzled people who'd never previously paid much attention to stock quotes. It's in the nature of news reporting that a story about a stock that went up by 1,000% attracts more eyeballs than one about an index that rose by 50%. Based on that sort of emphasis, many novice investors conclude that they can strike it rich by putting all of their modest savings into the next company that will fly off the charts. The only remaining detail is identifying that company.

This mindset sounds hopelessly naïve to longtime investors, who have seen countless past highfliers suddenly crash to earth. But the idea that *some* company will pay off in a huge and lasting way is not only plausible, but almost inevitable. Every so often, a spectacular technological breakthrough creates the potential for astronomical earnings growth at companies that successfully commercialize it.

In an earlier generation, "finding the next Xerox" was the aspiration of working stiffs with a dollar and a dream of joining the ranks of the idle rich. Xerox's patented photocopying process revolutionized office work. Its share price rose 15-fold from mid-1961, when Xerox listed on the New York Stock Exchange, through mid-1965. Even that gain paled next to the stock's appreciation during its pre-NYSE days. All told, from its 1949 low point to its all-time high in 1999, XRX's price increased 4,500-fold.

Many more superstar stocks have come down the pike since then. Reaping huge trading profits didn't always require patience. For example, Cisco's shares gained 195% in 1991. In 1999, Oracle's stock price advanced by 289%. In 1998, Amazon shares appreciated by a mind-boggling 967%.

Neither were sensational short-run price surges restricted to the high-tech sector. Tractor Supply shot up by

301% in 2001. Three years later, Monster Beverage racked up a one-year gain of 332%.

When I first started devoting $50 out of every paycheck to investing in stocks, I wasn't counting on such spectacular one-shot results. My business school education, my training as a trader, and my studies toward obtaining the Chartered Financial Analyst designation all emphasized grinding out steady but modest gains by closely studying a number of different securities.

Then, around 1983, I gained an insight into the bolder approach. At the time, I was serving as my alumni club's vice president for programs. I scheduled a presentation by a financial advisor who laid out a thoughtful plan for patiently building net worth over a lifetime. The key elements included diligently saving money, dollar-averaging into the market, limiting year-to-year swings by owning a balanced portfolio, and being conscious of taxes on income and capital gains.

At the conclusion, one club member expressed utter contempt for what he'd heard. "This sort of thing won't enable you to change your lifestyle," he sneered. To do that, he made clear to me, the attendees would have to invest in more speculative, private investments. He just so happened to deal in that sort of thing professionally.

That thumbs-down review of my speaker selection didn't trigger any radical change in my investment approach. In my personal investing and later, as a professional money manager, I continued to rely on a time-tested principle: Build your wealth over the long haul by owning a piece of the growing global economy.

The evidence is clear: By avoiding the mirage of trying to time the market and by staying away from fads, it's possible to accumulate a hefty nest egg for retirement. How big that nest egg will be depends largely on how much income you save and invest, year in and year out. If astute stock picks make that wealth grow at a somewhat higher rate than the market averages, so much the better.

But my fellow alum's concept of making a big enough bundle to fund a lifestyle change drove home an essential point: The security-minded middle-income couples portrayed on brokerage house and investment firms' commercials constitute only a portion of the investing public. A significant minority fantasizes about fifty-million-dollar houses and five-hundred-thousand-dollar cars. Immediately, if you please. Those speculators' hopes are smashed to smithereens every time the market pulls back from a delirious top. But come the next astronomic rise, another generation of newbies is there to chase the same get-rich-quick dream. And even some who got burned the last time around are convinced they'll make it work this time.

This is an aspect of human behavior that extends beyond stock market manias such as the 1990s dotcom frenzy. When home prices boomed in the 2000s, the dream of homeownership morphed into swiftly parlaying a small stake into a fortune in residential real estate. If this sounds about as feasible as becoming a centimillionaire by employing a "system" to beat the horseracing oddsmakers, that's no coincidence.

Think of the common phrase, "playing the market." That one was around long before self-appointed defenders of the public welfare began decrying the "gamification of investing." Concentrating your entire portfolio in a single stock, expecting that it will hit paydirt and change your lifestyle, doesn't differ in any important way from betting all your chips on a number on the roulette wheel. Federal Reserve Chairman Alan Greenspan had good reason, in 1999, to liken buying a red-hot Internet stock to hoping to hit the one-in-a-million lottery jackpot.

On the other hand, not all of those bettors you see in a casino are putting their lifesavings on the line. Many just find it entertaining to play blackjack or feed money into a slot machine for a few hours. They realize it'll probably cost them a couple of hundred bucks, but there's always a chance they'll get lucky.

The point is that not everybody is truly risk-averse, as financial textbooks generally assume. Some people get psychic pleasure from taking a chance. It's especially enticing if there's an intellectual challenge involved. When it comes to financial risk, the challenge is to find a way to channel the thrill-seeking into a harmless sort of activity. "Harmless" in this context means, "In the worst case, it's not going to cost you more than you might spend on some other form of excitement."

No less an authority than Wharton professor emeritus of finance Jeremy Siegel has said of the meme stocks, "I always recommend to young people, if you want to play with 10% or 15% of your portfolio in those games, fine. But, put the other 85% into some sort of an indexed long-term fund."[2] In my judgment, 10% or 15% is much more than is necessary to satisfy the speculative urge. Neither are index funds the only responsible choice for the remaining 98% or 99%. But Siegel's comment acknowledges the reality that investors aren't emotionless automatons with computers for brains, as a lot of financial research depicts them.

No matter how many studies our universities pump out to demonstrate the improbability of outwitting the supposedly perfect equity market, some investors are going to have an occasional fling with a stock that just might turn out to be the Big One. If they're wise, they'll subdue any urge to bet the farm on the proposition. The question then becomes, how should they go about trying to identify that killer stock?

You're unlikely to find a satisfying answer in Wall Street research. Sure, the analysts who write those reports are generally very bright. They're extremely knowledgeable about the industries they follow. But what use are they putting that all that IQ and knowledge to?

Their primary job is helping institutional clients beat the market average. Those portfolio managers don't have to beat it by a lot. A portfolio manager who consistently finishes in the top half of all managers every year will wind up in the top 25%. Sustained outperformance of this kind brings in additional dollars to manage, whether from pension plans, endowments, high-net-worth individuals, or mutual fund customers. Amassing more assets under management means more fee income.

The organizations competing in this system aren't about to risk their money machines on a single stock that might soar into the stratosphere, but could also go into a nosedive. Professional money managers perk up when a Wall Street analyst upgrades a stock from "Market Perform" to "Outperform" or boosts the price target by 10%. They're not looking for a "King of All Stocks" recommendation. They spread their risk over a lot of different stocks. Ideally, those stocks' returns will average out to something greater than the index's return. But what they need to avoid at all costs is getting so deep in a hole that it'll take them years to get back to even with the market.

So if you've set your sights on picking the #1 stock, conventional research reports will be useful only in a limited, specialized way. They'll help you get the operating lowdown on companies that you've already identified as candidates for the #1 slot. The first step, before you start digging into research reports, is to figure out which stocks most resemble the ones that topped the performance tables in the past. That's not a priority for stock analysis, but it's the primary focus of *The Little Book of Picking Top Stocks*.

To be clear: This book isn't designed to push readers into swinging for the fences, if they aren't already inclined to. I'm telling, not selling. But by learning about the very best-performing stocks, you'll gain insights into market dynamics that will make you a better investor.

In fact, if you belong to an investment club, or simply enjoy talking about stocks with your friends, here's an idea to try out: Toward the end of each year, have everyone name the S&P 500 stock they expect to be the coming year's top performer. Let everybody put a few dollars in a kitty, with the prize winner receiving a gift certificate or dinner at a nice restaurant. Participants can also buy a few shares of their nominated stocks if they wish.

Judging by historical experience, you'll still do pretty well if your pick comes in only #5 for the year or even #50. But your biggest benefit will come from doing the research. Going about it in a systematic way, based on what you'll learn in the following pages, will sharpen your skills for the more important task of creating a portfolio that's both responsible and profitable.

Plan of Attack

As experienced anglers will tell you, if you want to catch a fish, you have to go where the fish are. If your objective is to find next year's *numero uno*, don't waste time on stocks that are unlike any stock that's ever topped the total return table. The trick is to eliminate as many stocks from consideration as possible. Narrowing the list to a handful of candidates won't guarantee that you'll select the ultimate winner, but it will improve your odds tremendously.

I'll start by describing the pitfalls of relying primarily on conventional equity research when you're trying to land the stock market equivalent of a thousand-pound marlin. Then I'll tell the stories of past #1 stocks. Next, I'll describe several quantitative screens that can help you separate the minnows from the sharks. I'll also dispose of some logical-sounding selection techniques that can only put you off the track. And I'll isolate the qualitative characteristics that have distinguished top stocks of the past. I'll focus primarily on the stocks listed in Table P.1 and particularly on the leaders of the last five years shown.

The result of this painstaking study won't be a simple quantitative formula that's guaranteed to pick the #1 stock

Table P.1 #1 S&P 500 Stocks—2012–2021

Year	Stock	Return %
2012	PULTEGROUP INC.	188
2013	NETFLIX INC.	298
2014	SOUTHWEST AIRLINES CO.	126
2015	NETFLIX INC.	134
2016	NVIDIA CORP.	227
2017	NRG ENERGY INC.	134
2018	ADVANCED MICRO DEVICES	80
2019	ADVANCED MICRO DEVICES	148
2020	TESLA INC.	743
2021	DEVON ENERGY CORP.	196

Source: Bloomberg.

every year. If such a formula could be found, every investor would use it. By crowding into that targeted stock, they'd drive up its start-of-the-year price to a level that would leave only a mediocre potential for further gains. But by applying a mixture of quantitative criteria and qualitative factors that the market leaders have in common, you'll be fishing in a very select spot where the biggest fish are usually found.

Don't interpret "qualitative factors" to mean vague, squishy characteristics. A while back, a professor of technology and innovation at one of the world's highest-ranked business schools told me about a company that had caught his attention. He said it satisfied every one of his carefully defined criteria for spotting enterprises that were likely to succeed in a big way. I bought the stock, and it wound up being not only the S&P 500's #1 performer that year, but also the top performer among all #1 stocks in this book's 10-year study period. The company was Tesla and its shares gained 743% in 2020.

You shouldn't count on raking in that sort of profit every time you set out to find a top stock. And as I've already noted, it's not a good idea to funnel a large percentage of your wealth into just one stock with the expectation of making enough in the space of 12 months to retire for life. But neither do you need to pick a name out of a hat and hope for a miracle. If finding the way to #1 intrigues you, you can attempt it in a calculating, evidence-based way. Read on to learn how.

Acknowledgments

———— ∽ ————

THIS BOOK WOULD NOT have become a reality without John Lee's devotion to tracking down and testing voluminous data. I am grateful to Bill Falloon and Purvi Patel of John Wiley & Sons for their roles in getting the project approved and seeing it through to the finished product. My thanks as well to Fernando Alvarez, Peter Ernster, Steven Miller, Barry Nelson, Megan Neuberger, Daniel Partlow, Eric Rosenthal, Dominique Terris, and the dedicated staff of the Baker Library at Harvard Business School for helping to make the book as good as it could be. Above all, Elaine Sisman has earned my deepest gratitude for her unwavering encouragement and advice.

Chapter One

Forget About Conventional Analysis

~

SEEKING A PROFESSIONAL'S OPINION makes sense in lots of situations. Say you're about to agree to buy a house. If you don't happen to be an engineer who specializes in judging structural soundness and safety, it might be a good idea to hire someone with that expertise to look the place over. Or suppose you can afford a painting by a famous artist to hang on a wall in that house, but you don't know the art market well. You'd be wise to pay a consultant who can tell you where comparable works sell at auction.

It might seem to follow that if you're trying to pick next year's #1 stock, you'd want to look for it in research produced by people who analyze stocks for a living. Equity analysts employed at Wall Street firms or independent research organizations know the companies they follow inside out, thanks to specializing by industry and concentrating on a small number of stocks. Over many years of studying their industries, they've developed valuable contacts at their companies' suppliers and customers.

As a result, analysts often know what's happening on the ground before it shows up in earnings reports or newspaper articles. What's more, these stock evaluators process vast amounts of data. That complements the judgment they've developed through lengthy experience. Most Wall Street equity analysts are also extremely bright. And you can learn exactly which of these brainy and highly motivated analysts are considered the best in their field, thanks to annual surveys and scorekeeping by various organizations, most famously by *Institutional Investor*.

Despite those assurances, do you want to run the top analysts' top picks through one more battery of tests? No problem. Their recommendations, which are based on "fundamental" factors such as companies' competitive strength and earnings prospects, are complemented by "technical" analysis that's conducted by a separate group of highly intelligent professionals. Also known as "chartists," they make predictions about stocks' future movements based on statistical relationships between price trends from one period to the next.

No doubt about it, there's a lot of intellectual firepower for you to draw on as you attempt to identify the year's highest-return stock before it takes off for the moon. The question is whether any of it is useful in that quest. I'm not disputing the value of the skills that enable premier analysts to command big-time compensation packages. It's just that the system they're part of isn't geared toward the objective that's the focus of this book.

From Earnings Forecasts to Recommendations

A typical Wall Street equity research department includes specialized analysts covering a wide array of industries—high-tech, low-tech, financials, commodities producers, consumer goods, business-to-business, and more. The competitive dynamics of those industries vary tremendously, but the analysts boil their work down to a uniform, easy-to-understand set of acronyms.

Each analyst projects the company's earnings for the coming year and divides that amount by number of shares outstanding to produce an earnings per share (EPS) estimate. Dividing the company's share price by its projected EPS produces the price-earnings (PE) multiple. PE multiples are also calculated with trailing-twelve-months EPS as the denominator.

PE multiples vary according to companies' perceived earnings quality and expected future EPS growth rate. The analyst assigned to a given company renders an opinion on what its PE ought to be, based on how it stacks up on those factors against other companies in its industry. Multiplying the company's "correct" PE multiple by its projected EPS produces a price target (PT).

Based on where the stock's current price stands relative to its PT, the analyst assigns a rating to the stock. The ratings terminology varies by firm, but the most straightforward set-up consists of a Buy, Hold, or Sell recommendation. Other firms' language emphasizes how a stock is likely to do relative to a market index, using designations such as "Outperform" and "Market Weight." But regardless of the terminology, the investor can examine a full list of a firm's recommendations and determine which stock has the biggest upside, based on where it stands in comparison to its PT. This is all founded, keep in mind, on the critical task of projecting the company's EPS.

There's just one small problem.

The Irrelevance of EPS

Almost half a century before this book's publication, the distinguished financial economist Joel Stern demonstrated that EPS has no bearing on stock prices. Stern's findings weren't by any means buried in obscurity and forgotten. His article "Earnings per Share Don't Count"[1] appeared in the widely read *Financial Analysts Journal* of July–August 1974, and it was actively discussed at Harvard Business School, which I entered the following month. (Warning: The next eight paragraphs are more technical than the rest of this book's content. You can skip lightly over the discussion if you're willing to accept Stern's findings on the grounds that they passed muster with the editors of a leading scholarly journal. The *Financial Analysts Journal* is now the flagship publication of the Chartered Financial Analysts' organization.)

The fallacy of regarding a company's share price as a function of its EPS can be seen by considering a fictitious PFDZ Corp., which is earning a solid 15% return on its fixed capital. (Fixed capital includes assets such as property, plant, and equipment.) Thanks to its strong profitability, the company has a high credit rating that enables it to borrow at a 4% interest rate. PFDZ can substantially increase its EPS by borrowing money to make a large investment that will return anything in excess of 4%. I'll make it 5% for the sake of argument.

How will the market respond to learning that PFDZ, which previously earned 15% on fixed capital, expects to earn just 5% on its new investments? Let's just say the news won't be received warmly. And as Stern points out, the market will reduce the PE multiple on PFDZ's EPS to reflect the increase in its financial leverage, that is, its reliance on borrowed money. In short, EPS will increase, but XYZ's share price won't. It may even decline.

Here's another way to demonstrate the EPS fallacy suggested by Stern: Consider two companies, NWRQ and YMDO. Both earned $1.00 a share in the latest 12 months and both are expected to grow their earnings at 10% a year. Neither company has any debt on its balance sheet and neither intends to use debt in the future. Based on what you know so far, you'd expect the two companies' shares to sell at the same PE multiple. Let's assume that's 20×, meaning that NWRQ and YMDO shares are both trading at $20.

But now let's add one more piece of information. NWRQ can achieve its 10% earnings growth without needing to add to its present capital. It's an "asset-lite" company that generates sales primarily from the brainpower of software developers whose office space and computer terminals are already in place. YMDO, on the other hand, will need one additional dollar of capital for each additional dollar of sales it must generate in order to increase its earnings. Where will YMDO get that additional capital? Having ruled out the use of debt, the company has just two possible sources.

One possibility for YMDO is to sell additional shares to fund the investments required to produce the projected 10% earnings increase over the next 12 months. In that case, YMDO's earnings will be spread out over a larger number of shares than formerly. Its EPS will go down, relative to the EPS of NWRQ, which won't need to issue any more shares. If EPS is truly the basis on which the market prices stocks, then on a forward-multiple basis, NWRQ's shares must carry a higher price today than YMDO's shares, yet in fact they're both currently at $20.

The other way YMDO can raise the capital it requires to increase its earnings is by reinvesting some of its earnings in the business. NWRQ, on the other hand, can pay out all of its earnings to shareholders as a dividend. Reviewing the facts, would you really pay as much for YMDO's stock, with equivalent current-year EPS and projected earnings growth as NWRQ but with a smaller dividend?

Alternatively, NWRQ can return 100% of its earnings to shareholders by repurchasing stock. That will reduce its number of shares outstanding and increase its EPS over the next 12 months. If YMDO tries to follow the same strategy, it will have less money to spend on stock repurchases because it needs to reinvest some of its earnings in its business. Compared to NWRQ, YMDO will have more shares outstanding a year from now and less projected EPS. Once again, the market will put a lower price on its shares than on NWRQ's today, even if it applies the same 20 times PE multiple to both companies' projected EPS. Yet that contradicts the original premise that both stocks are currently trading at $20.

Clearly, it's impossible for NWRQ and YMDO to trade at both the same price and at different prices at the same time. Stern untangles this paradox with an inescapable conclusion: The market doesn't really value shares on the basis of EPS. What it really cares about is, in Stern's words, "earnings net of the amount of capital required to be invested in order to maintain an expected rate of growth in profits." He dubbed this metric *free cash flow*. The Corporate Finance Institute defines free cash flow as Operating Cash Flow – Capital Expenditures.

Stern laid out these irrefutable facts nearly 50 years before this book went to press. Yet to this day, as Hans Wagner lamented in a 2022 *Investopedia* article, "very few people look at how much free cash flow (FCF) is available vis-à-vis the value of the company."[2] But that's not surprising, given the massive volume of equity research that's pumped out every year with a single-minded focus on EPS. Investors who are trained to repeat the formula

"Price equals EPS times PE" aren't especially inclined to muddy the waters with FCF.

EPS: Flawed but Dominant

As Stern commented in his 1974 article, "That EPS is easy to calculate is an insufficient excuse for employing it as an analytical device."[3] Certainly, simplicity is no justification for relying on a measure that doesn't truly reflect how stocks are evaluated by the sophisticated investors ("lead steers") who, according to Stern, ultimately determine prices. And it's not unusual to see the market ignore the message supposedly delivered when a company reports an EPS number that beats analysts' consensus forecast. Instead of rising, the stock sometimes falls because something else in the report represents a disappointment, such as revenue, gross margin, or the company's earnings guidance for the next period.

EPS nevertheless remains entrenched in Wall Street equity research and understandably so. Imagine that you're an industry-specialized equity analyst trying to make your mark by recommending a stock that you think will hugely outpace the index over the next year. It's awfully hard to come up with that kind of a pick when your industry is massively out of favor and likely to remain so for the next several quarters. But in the meantime, you have a chance to shine every three months. If you can precisely predict quarterly EPS for one of your companies, you'll have your moment of stardom. Never mind that the number may have a loose relationship with the underlying economic reality. EPS is routinely massaged by a variety of discretionary and arbitrary accounting decisions to achieve management's desired result. But only short-sellers care much about make-believe earnings numbers.

Aside from the gratification that comes from sometimes hitting the number on the nose, it makes sense for equity analysts to put lots of energy into predicting 90-day batches of EPS. Various organizations compile analysts' EPS estimates to generate the consensus forecasts that I mentioned a few paragraphs back. Being included in those compilations certifies a brokerage house or independent research firm as a thought leader. If that's how the game is played, it's in the analyst's interest to help the firm's research director fill in the EPS box for every company under coverage. To get along, go along, as the saying goes. (Not that providing an EPS forecast is optional.)

Simplicity helps to explain why EPS takes on such great importance in Wall Street's equity research machine. But EPS prediction has also intrigued finance professors, who are far from intimidated by complexity. They've done studies on such questions as why analysts' estimates are biased in the direction of excessive optimism[4] and how analyst incentives lead to forecast errors.[5] Another study found that 40% of the time, an EPS forecast derived from a time series of past data was as accurate or more accurate than the analysts' consensus forecast.[6]

The question of what causes a particular S&P 500 stock to outperform all 499 of its peers isn't the sort of question that financial scholars tend to take up. Quite reasonably, they're more inclined to ask something like the following: "Within that group of 500 stocks, can I find some characteristic that enables me to select 100 that, on average, will beat the index?"

If those stocks collectively return 1% more than the index, with some doing better and some doing worse, and this is shown to be a statistically valid result rather than a chance outcome, then the study has a good chance of getting published in a prestigious journal. That may help the author become a tenured professor or, in the case of someone who's already attained that status, to attract an offer to move to a rival university at a higher salary. The methodology described in the study may even get adopted as one of the strategies employed by an institutional investment manager with the necessary resources to select and monitor hundreds of stocks at a time.

The point is that the finance departments of the world's business schools produce a large volume of genuinely useful research every year. But it's not directed at the investor who's attempting to do something financial theorists don't believe a rational individual would try to do. That is, trying to find the needle in the haystack that may double your money or more within the next 12 months.

The theoreticians might be less astounded if you explain that you're allocating just a minor portion of your portfolio to trying to hit the jackpot. And in the meantime, you're investing most of your self-managed 401(k) in the more prudent, well-diversified manner they approve of as a rational approach. But even if the finance professors are okay with that, they probably won't make your hunt for #1 the subject of their next research study. Their chances of getting published in a prestigious journal are higher if they stick to the topics that the journals have focused on in the past.

EPS versus Underlying Reality

The equity research establishment's overreliance on EPS might be more excusable if earnings invariably represented a genuine creation of economic value on behalf of shareholders. In practice, the gap between reported earnings and bona fide profits can be vast. Sometimes the mismatch reflects outright accounting fraud. But investors shouldn't be lulled into believing that they're getting the straight dope on a company's earnings merely because none of its executives are under indictment. Reported EPS can diverge from the underlying reality because of perfectly lawful accounting practices or because the numbers dispensed in quarterly financial statements are later said to have been mistakes.

Before we examine how companies present a distorted picture without violating any securities laws, let's get clear on why they routinely do it. The reason is that those who operate within the PE × EPS = Stock Price framework assume that obtaining a high multiple depends not only on achieving high growth, but also on achieving steady growth. All else being equal, they reckon, investors prefer EPS that climbs year by year at a steady clip to one that moves up in fits and starts. So between two otherwise similar stocks, the one with less volatile EPS should receive a higher PE multiple and deliver a higher return.

That, at least, is what corporate managers believe. But that's not what a 2013 study by Tim Koller, Bin Jiang, and Rishi Raj[7] concluded. Those researchers at the management consulting firm McKinsey found no statistically valid evidence that lower earnings volatility produces higher returns for shareholders.

But even if low-volatility earnings don't ultimately translate into superior investor returns, institutional investment managers may tell corporate managers that they prefer smooth over erratic earnings. Imagine a portfolio manager meeting with a client, a pension plan sponsor, for instance.

In a review of the portfolio's current holdings the client asks about a company that recently reported a big, unexpected drop in EPS from the year-earlier quarter. The resulting price drop has made the stock a conspicuous underperformer within a portfolio that wasn't doing especially well before this nasty surprise. Why, the client wants to know, didn't the portfolio manager foresee the trouble and reduce exposure to the stock?

This isn't a comfortable conversation for the portfolio manager. Striving to own companies that never rock the boat with negative earnings surprises may help to avoid such unpleasant interactions in the future. The message this portfolio manager is likely to convey in meetings with corporate managements and their investment bankers is, "We like companies that show nice, steady EPS progression."

Eager to get its stock into the portfolios of all the managers who deliver a similar message, the company can, if it chooses, try to accommodate their desire in perfectly legitimate ways that truly affect its economic performance. Suppose, for example, that a manufacturer uses as raw materials certain commodities that gyrate wildly in price from one quarter to the next. By hedging its raw materials costs in the futures market, the company can prevent those cost swings from making its earnings bounce around like a jumping bean.

Smoothing out input costs isn't the only way to produce smooth EPS growth. Broader corporate strategies can also take some of the volatility out of earnings. For example, companies in industries where revenues are closely tied to the business cycle might diversify into others that hold up better in recessions.

Working at various investment banks over the years, I saw senior management deal with the boom-and-bust nature of the commission business. A hot market stoked the public's interest in the stock market, with the result that trading volume and commissions went up. But boom turned to bust when the market slumped. To even out those swings, the investment banks sought to concentrate more of their revenues in steadier, fee-based activities. Asset management was one such activity. Instead of depending on customers to make trades and pay commissions, the firms managed the customers' portfolios for a fee calculated as a percentage of aggregate portfolio value.

Portfolio values were subject to ups and downs, but management fees were still a stabler source of revenue than commissions. The attractiveness of that proposition helped investment banks overcome their hesitancy about doing something they had to think long and hard about. Entering the fee-based management business meant going into competition with the asset managers who were their customers on the institutional side.

It's important to note that the McKinsey authors mentioned earlier don't recommend realigning corporate revenues in pursuit of steadier EPS progression. But that's exactly what some companies do. They attempt to reduce their earnings volatility through diversifying acquisitions. The idea is that industries have different business cycles, so one business line's peak earnings will offset the trough at another's.

It sounds good in theory, but it doesn't work out so well in practice. Koller, Jiang, and Raj found that of the 50 S&P 500 companies with the lowest earnings volatility over a 10-year period, fewer than 10 were diversified, as defined by owning businesses in more than two distinct businesses. Furthermore, the McKinsey experts uncovered no evidence that low-earning-volatility companies commanded premium prices. They reported that in their experience, the sum of the values of diversified companies' businesses almost never differed materially from the market values of their stocks.

The McKinsey researchers conducted their study in a period long after the breakup of most of the famous conglomerates that were created in the 1960s partly on the premise of reducing earnings volatility through diversification. Those companies' experience supports the view that in terms of market value, the whole was less than the sum of the parts. Their stocks traded with a "conglomerate discount."

The discount was so substantial that corporate raiders were able to pay a premium to a conglomerate's prevailing stock price, gain control, and then sell or spin off the distinct operations and come away with a handsome profit. In these cases, the original conglomerate builders' plan to obtain high PE multiples by minimizing EPS volatility achieved the opposite effect. They set out to make 2 + 2 equal 5 but instead created a total of 3.

So much for the available methods of reducing volatility in quarterly earnings reports by actually addressing the underlying reality. When those methods don't accomplish everything management had hoped for—probably because no business actually grows by the same percentage year in and year out, much less quarter to quarter—there are ways to create the *appearance* of earnings stability without breaking any laws.

Imagine that a company's sales get a sudden boost in its second quarter thanks to a temporary surge in demand or a few unusually large orders. This might sound like good news, but in a world of EPS-obsessed traders, analysts, and portfolio managers it can present a problem. Suppose there's little chance that the company's windfall will be repeated in next year's second quarter. What's likely to happen if, as a result of the short-term factors, the company reports second-quarter earnings that are substantially above trendline? Twelve months from now management could find itself in the unenviable position of having to report a sub-normal year-over-year second-quarter earnings increase, even though business is going fine. If that happens, those stability-conscious portfolio managers may become disenchanted and reduce their positions in the stock. Their liquidations could depress the share price, a bad outcome for the CEO, whose bonus is tied to it.

Luckily for the CEO, there's a solution. Just accelerate some of the regular maintenance work scheduled for the third quarter to the second quarter. With an extra quarter's worth of that expense booked in the second quarter, second-quarter earnings won't be far above trendline. So it will be possible to report the desired year-over-year percentage gain in next year's second quarter.

The benefits of the short-run demand boom won't be lost. They'll just be more conveniently timed. Result: No stock hiccup next year and no damage to the CEO's bonus from too much of a good thing. Too bad for serious investors who are just trying to get an accurate picture of the company's performance.

Naturally, problems in producing the steady growth of EPS that helps everyone except the investors can arise from events that cause quarterly earnings to be too low rather than too high. When that happens, "channel-stuffing" can come to the rescue for companies that sell products through distributors or wholesalers. These companies ring up sales when the middlemen buy their products, not when a sale is made to the ultimate consumer. So if sales look like they're going to fall a little short in the current quarter, it's just a matter of getting the distributors or wholesalers to buy a little earlier than they had planned. That way, the company can count some sales in this quarter rather than the next. It's a practice otherwise known as borrowing sales from a future period.

There's a potential snag in this remedy, however. The distributors that accept delivery earlier than usual have to hold above-normal amounts of goods in inventory until the sell-through to their customers brings those inventory levels back down. That increases the cost of financing their inventories. While they might be glad to lend a hand in the manufacturer's effort to present a misleadingly smooth earnings progression, they're not necessarily willing to reduce their own profits in the process. Consequently, the manufacturer may have to persuade them to play ball by offering them a discount in exchange for taking delivery ahead of the usual schedule.

The revenue that the manufacturer sacrifices in this arrangement isn't revenue that it will make up later. It's lost forever. And it's not the result of a discount offered for a legitimate business purpose, such as clearing out stale merchandise. Instead, the discount's purpose is purely cosmetic, namely, creating the illusion of a rock-steady rate of increase in EPS. Creating genuine economic value has taken a back seat to manufacturing numbers that just make it *look like* the company is creating economic value.

A further step into the realm of financial reporting fantasy involves *arbitrary timing of discretionary accounting decisions.* That phrase may sound like gobbledygook, but what it represents is easy to understand. Suppose, for example, that a company does have some stale merchandise in its inventory. At some point, it will have to write down that value of those goods to a level that represents prices it can now realistically expect to obtain. But there's some judgment involved in determining exactly when the merchandise's current carrying stops being a realistic number.

Management's professional judgment is that the current quarter isn't the best time to come to that conclusion. By an incredibly amazing coincidence, earnings are threatening to come in a bit below trendline this quarter. Taking a write-down at this particular time would worsen that problem.

Everything points to a profit rebound a couple to quarters from now. In fact, at that point EPS will be in danger of going too far *above* trendline. Upon very careful consideration, management concludes that the loss of value on that stale merchandise will become indisputable just about six months from. So that's when the company will take the write-down.

Another type of loss that companies can book when it's most convenient is a write-off of bad receivables. These are amounts owed by customers who bought on credit but, as it turns out, won't be able to pay what they owe. Also, management can exercise judgment in deciding when to write off goodwill.

By way of explanation, goodwill is a balance sheet item that arises when a company makes an acquisition for more than the accounting-based fair value of the acquired company's net assets. Suppose the acquisition doesn't work out as hoped. In that case, the acquiring company must eventually acknowledge that the value it expected to create by combining the acquired company's operations with its own never materialized.

A different way for a manipulative management to exploit acquisitions is to make a subjective judgment that some of the receivables of the company being acquired will never be collected. Writing them off at the outset, before they can affect the acquirer's earnings, sounds like management is acting responsibly. But the acquirer may go even further and write off some receivables that actually aren't so bad. Later on, the company can collect those good receivables and record a gain, producing earnings as if out of thin air.

These examples don't by any means exhaust the range of non-illegal gimmicks that companies have devised over the years for manipulating their earnings. In his heyday in the 1980s and 1990s, General Electric's legendary Jack Welch was determined to make EPS rise at a steady rate every quarter, come rain or come shine. Every division of the company was expected to do its part.

An executive in GE's financial services business recounted that if quarter-end was approaching and divisional earnings were in danger of falling short of their target, he and his colleagues would scramble to find an acquisition. The acquired company's earnings could be counted for the full quarter, enabling the division to meet its quota. It's not unreasonable to suppose that GE's selection of acquisition targets would have been different if it had been based strictly on maximizing the company's long-run economic value, instead of satisfying Wall Street's demands for an ultra-smooth earnings progression.

Hooray! There's Less Accounting Fraud Than There Used to Be

Up to this point, I've described only techniques for artificially reporting steady EPS growth that don't violate the accounting rules and land senior management in the slammer. There's some good news on this front for investors who want to know what's actually going on at companies. I mean the ones who aren't interested in playing the game of seeing whether the company beat analysts' forecasts of a manipulated number that has no real bearing on the stock price. The good news is that outright financial fraud has become less frequent in the United States over the past several years.

Is it necessary to add that this wasn't the result of CEOs suddenly deciding that collecting big bonuses based on their stocks' performance was less important than providing a true and transparent picture of their companies' performance? No, the real reason that making stuff up became a less favored tactic is that the Sarbanes-Oxley Act of 2002 made it harder for the CEO to shift the blame for fraud to subordinates.

That law required CEOs to sign the financial statements that their companies submitted to the Securities and Exchange Commission. Previously, a CEO could get away with implausibly claiming that the fraud was entirely the Chief Financial Officer's doing, even if that executive's bonus plan wasn't tied in any way to the company's stock performance. In that case, the CFO had no obvious motive for falsifying the financial results.

By the way, Congress's largely successful effort to suppress financial reporting fraud was a response to several high-profile cases, most famously the collapse of Enron. That epidemic of accounting crimes, in turn, resulted from an earlier shift in executive compensation practices. In the old days, boards of directors evaluated CEOs' performance on the basis of EPS, rather than stock performance. This enabled CEOs to game the system with accounting changes that did nothing to increase shareholder value.

For example, suppose a manufacturer had some equipment for which it had determined the useful life to be seven years. Each year, one-seventh of the machine's purchase price would be deducted from the company's reported earnings, until it was regarded as having no remaining value due to wear-and-tear or obsolescence. (This treatment for reporting to shareholders is known as "straight-line depreciation.") In the separate and different set of financial statements submitted to the Internal Revenue Service, the company would write off more than one-seventh per year in the early years, in order to obtain bigger tax deductions.

The CEO would get the engineers and accountants together and ask whether eight years wouldn't be a more realistic estimate of the machine's useful life. Surely some justification for the change could be found. Especially given that the CEO had a big say in the engineers' and accountants' compensation and promotion. The revised accounting treatment would produce a smaller annual depreciation charge, meaning earnings would go up. Serendipitously, so would the CEO's performance-based bonus.

Research studies found that the market saw through this charade. The resulting increase in EPS wasn't mirrored by any increase in free cash flow, the metric that Joel Stern had found was the true driver of stock valuations. Consequently, the CEO-instigated rejiggering of the numbers didn't push the stock price higher. It merely fattened the CEO's bonus, which was based on a severely flawed, highly manipulable measure of corporate financial performance.

Boards of directors, to their credit, began to recognize the flaw in their previous approach. They saw that CEOs were taking advantage of the EPS-based compensation plans. Instead of increasing shareholders' wealth with actions that would boost the stock price, CEOs were extracting money from shareholders in the form of inflated bonuses.

In the name of "aligning shareholder and management interests," corporations shifted to bonus plans geared to stock price performance. Going forward, bonuses would be paid in stock options that would gain in value if the share price rose, making the company's owners better off. No more would the CEO benefit from accounting ploys that added nothing to FCF.

One might have thought, amid this awakening to contrived EPS increases that had no effect on share prices, equity analysts would have revised their methods as well. Some research organizations did in fact incorporate more sophisticated analysis into their reports. But a noteworthy counterexample stands out in my memory.

The incident resulted from the Financial Accounting Standards Board (FASB, pronounced "fazz-bee") announcing a rule change that was to take effect the following year.

Unlike the changes in accounting practices that individual CEOs brought about at their respective companies, the new standard applied to all companies. But it, too, had no effect on companies' cash flows, instead changing only how quickly certain expenses hit their income statements.

Because I was known to have an interest in the topic, I was pulled into a discussion of the revised accounting standard. One equity analyst expressed enthusiasm for the new rule. "Earnings will rise by 10% at all of my companies," he exulted. "I'm raising my valuations across the board."

I pointed out that FASB's rule revision's impact was purely cosmetic, as it left companies' cash flows untouched. The analyst clearly had no idea what I was talking about. Having previously worked in the industry that he now covered, he understood his companies' operations inside out. But his grasp of accounting went only as far as being able to calculate EPS. His mastery of equity valuation began and ended at PE × EPS = PT.

In contrast, the CEOs quickly grasped the implications for their compensation of boards' new emphasis on stock price performance over pliable EPS numbers. The response of the more unscrupulous among them was to resort to outright fraud. Instead of monkeying around with depreciation schedules, they manipulated EPS in a way the market couldn't see through, namely, creating totally fictitious earnings. This had the intended effect of raising their companies' stock prices, at least until the schemes collapsed and criminal charges were filed. So many scandals erupted that, for a time, stock prices in general were depressed as investors wondered whether any company's stated earnings were reliable.

The 2002 "Sarbox" law cut down significantly on outright accounting fraud at U.S. companies. But even today, investors aren't completely out of danger in the form of PE multiples getting applied to largely imaginary EPS numbers. Clever CEOs have managed to dodge the prospect of 10-year prison terms (20 years if the misconduct is found to be willful) through a gimmick known as "subcertification." The CEOs require lower-level employees to affirm the accuracy of the financial statements. Then, the CEOs merely certify that if those affirmations are correct, the reported numbers are accurate. As a result, there haven't been many Sarbox-based prosecutions or convictions of CEOs for faking the earnings.

Even the reduction, as opposed to elimination, of sensational financial reporting frauds in the United States has significantly cut down the number of attractive targets for short sellers who specialize in scrutinizing companies' accounting practices. Fortunately, other countries have continued to provide them plenty of lucrative opportunities. And it's not as if the EPS figures reported by American companies always turn out to be correct.

Let's imagine a company reports quarterly EPS far in excess of analysts' consensus forecast. You quickly enter a Buy order for the stock, expecting that the market will now begin pricing it on the basis of higher expected earnings than formerly. And the stock does in fact rally, giving you a healthy profit. But several months later, the company says (I loosely paraphrase), "Oops! Those EPS numbers we gave you were too high, due to a mistake in our accounting department. Sorry about that." The share price plunges on the news, erasing your earlier gain.

You may have a suspicion that the initial, incorrect report wasn't genuinely the result of an error. A study by Joshua Livnat and Christine E.L. Tan of New York University's Stern School of Business Administration examined thousands of earnings restatements.[8] The authors found evidence that, as they diplomatically put it, "the originally reported earnings may have been strategically managed." *Investopedia* defines *earnings management* as "the use of accounting techniques to produce financial statements that present an overly positive view of a company's business activities and financial position."

Livnat and Tan reported that restatements occurred in only 3.4% of the 220,000 quarterly financial reports in their database. But that isn't necessarily a good enough reason to be complacent about the reliability of the EPS figures that Corporate America pumps out. Midway through 2021 the *Wall Street Journal* reported that more than 540 companies had restated earnings in the previous three months, an amount higher than in any full year since 2013.

The upsurge resulted from an SEC determination that many special-purpose acquisition companies (SPACs) were improperly accounting for warrants they'd issued in the course of raising capital. According to analysts, this development took the market by surprise. On top of that, some SPACs and companies acquired by them disclosed more serious accounting problems in their restatements. For example, Lordstown Motors Corp. said it had "substantial doubt" about its ability to finish the year as a going concern. The company's top two executives subsequently resigned over inaccurate recording of preorders for its electric trucks.

Aside from the specific case of SPACs, it's important to realize that restatements sometimes go beyond "correcting an error" in a recent quarter. In some cases, the company is forced to change reported earnings for every quarter in the last few years. The stock price can get hammered in the process.

Earnings versus Value Creation

Many investment pundits are so wedded to the fallacy that wealth is created when a company borrows two cents a share from next quarter's earnings to beat the analysts' consensus forecast that they deny the reality of billions of dollars of legitimate wealth creation in some of the world's most dynamic growth industries. They deride companies that have never reported a profit according to Generally Accepted Accounting Principles (GAAP, pronounced "gap"), yet are awarded with *market capitalizations* in the billions by allegedly deluded investors. ("Market cap" = Share Price × Total Number of Shares Outstanding.) These companies trade on multiples of sales rather than PE multiples, like normal ones. "It's the Dutch tulip craze all over again!" shout the naysayers.

Have there been examples of companies that went public with no bottom line, obtaining astronomical market valuations, only to crash and burn a few years later? Certainly. Did some of them have business models that didn't make a lot of sense, but rode the wave of a prevailing investment fad? Yes. Reasonable people can conclude that certain failed ventures fit the narrative. This is true despite the conviction of hardcore believers in *efficient markets*. (That's the notion that it's impossible to beat the stock averages on a risk-adjusted basis because stocks are always priced correctly.) But did every company that amassed a gigantic market capitalization without producing positive GAAP earnings prove to be a speculative bubble that burst, leaving its credulous investors in tears? Absolutely not.

Amazon (AMZN) can be considered the poster child for bona fide value that's unrelated to EPS. In its first several years after going public in 1997, the online retailer unfailingly reported losses. The first year in which it showed a GAAP profit was 2003. But before that "breakthrough" year began, Amazon had attained a $7.3 billion market capitalization. The graph shown in Figure 1.1 illustrates just how long it took for GAAP to catch up with the reality that Amazon was generating a substantial *economic profit*.

How were the allegedly gullible investors who bought AMZN punished for their supposed folly? By the end of 2021, the company's market capitalization had risen by more than 20,000% to $1.7 trillion. From the end of 2002 to the end of 2021, Amazon shareholders realized a 31.27% total return versus 11.49% for the S&P 500. If that's what a fool and his money soon being parted looks like, bring it on!

Here's what the Amazon bashers missed and what their present-day kindred spirits continue to miss: GAAP is an accounting system that's very well designed . . . for nineteenth-century manufacturing companies. Through most of the twentieth century, GAAP served investors in most industries reasonably well. But GAAP hasn't adapted well to the transformation of America's industrial base beginning in the 1990s. The problem arises from failing to acknowledge what constitutes an asset in this day and age.

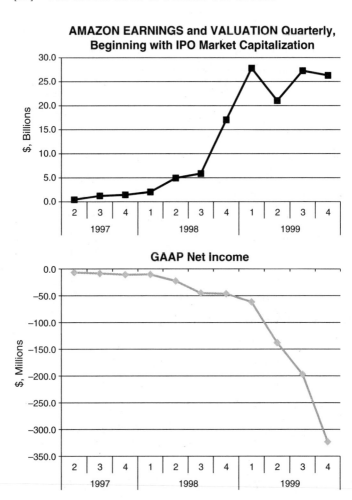

Figure 1.1 Amazon Historical Market Cap and Net Income
Source: Bloomberg LP.

In a correct, non-jargony way, Oracle Netsuite defines an asset as: "anything that has current or future economic value to a business." Here's what that means in practical terms: Suppose a textile mill circa 1850 buys a loom for $100. That $100 doesn't get counted as an expense. Instead, it goes into the asset column on the company's balance sheet. On the other hand, if the textile mill pays $100 in wages over a given period, that amount does get recorded as an expense, thereby reducing net income by $100.

According to GAAP, wages paid last month don't provide any ongoing economic value to the company. The mill has sold the cloth that the workers produced, so it will provide ongoing economic value to the mill's customers, not to the mill. The company will have to pay its workers again this month to produce more cloth. But the loom is still in service and providing value beyond the period in which the company shelled out the money for it.

Now let's consider an infotech company that spends $10 million in 2023 on designing a software package for small businesses. The project proves successful, the company copyrights the new software, and customers love it. In the first year, sales of the new product total $4 million, exceeding management's most optimistic expectations. Note that the company hasn't sold its ownership of the software package, only licenses to use it. Cash is flowing in, the owners are high-fiving each other, but the picture presented by the company's income statement is much less rosy.

Under the rules laid down by GAAP, the $10 million research expenditure was classified as an expense. That's despite the fact that the outlay produced something that definitely delivers current and future value to the business—a proprietary software package that will generate revenue for years to come. But according to GAAP, the company lost $6 million on the new software in 2023, before even taking into account the selling costs and corporate overhead.

Even more weirdly, if the product generates $6 million of sales in 2024, the company will report a substantial profit on the software package. Of course, that profit may get wiped out by the planned $12 million of research and development (R&D) expenditures on its next product, to be introduced in 2025. Still, the company is generating cash and all indications are that it will continue creating cash-generating products for the foreseeable future. If the founders decide to sell the company, the response they'll receive certainly won't be, "Your GAAP earnings are negative. *You'll* have to pay *me* to take this loser off your hands."

The distorted picture produced by GAAP-defined earnings wasn't an entirely new problem in 1995 or so. I first heard about it in business school in the mid-1970s, long before dotcoms and other asset-lite tech companies arrived on the scene. Then as now, pharmaceutical producers were creating enduring value for their businesses in the form of patented drugs. The huge numbers of R&D dollars expended on inventing those drugs were booked as expenses, rather than on the asset side of the companies' balance sheets. Sparse asset amounts relative to their liabilities meant that the pharmaceutical makers had less shareholders' equity than other industrial companies with comparable revenues.

Because of the modest amount of GAAP equity on their balance sheets, drug makers had exceptionally high ratios of net income to equity (return on equity, or ROE). Due to this mathematical quirk, pharmaceutical companies' ROE was conspicuously high among industrial companies. The industry's critics cited the numbers as purported evidence that drug companies were reaping unconscionably high profits by charging excessive prices on their desperately needed products. If GAAP had permitted them to treat patented drugs with ongoing benefits to their businesses as assets, politicians and the public would have gotten a very different—and more accurate—picture. But as you can imagine, explaining this arcane accounting issue was no simple task for the pharmaceutical industry's government affairs and public relations staffs.

For the drug industry, it was a problem that GAAP was wiping out sources of ongoing value that were assets in all but name. But this wasn't a concern for most other companies. Shortly before the dawn of the present millennium, however, the problem began to become more widespread. Certainly, the S&P 500 still included lots of companies that depended on physical capital to bend metal or sell merchandise off store shelves. But over the next several years Corporate America's ranks were increasingly populated by companies that relied primarily on brain power to produce digital entertainment or to recruit social network users.

One likely response to the idea of treating a *New Economy* company's intellectual property as an asset is, "That's not something I can touch and feel, like an oil refinery or a truck fleet." But it's eminently feasible, outside of the GAAP world, to assign values to these non-physical assets. For example, cable or satellite television subscribers pay a known subscription fee and on average continue as subscribers for a determinable number of years. Those predictable future revenues can be converted into an asset value by well-established financial methodology.

In fact, it's common nowadays for companies to supplement the GAAP numbers that they're required to report with adjusted numbers. These are meant to help investors understand businesses that don't quite fit the mold of conventional securities analysis. The alternative measures include adjusted versions of EPS. In many cases, analysts place primary emphasis on the adjusted EPS, rather than the GAAP version.

Unfortunately, companies can craft their own versions of adjusted financial ratios. Without the standardization that's one virtue of GAAP, comparing companies becomes difficult. And comparing companies' financial results and valuations is an essential component of securities analysis. But if companies with a vested interest in putting the best possible face on their financial performance start tinkering with a measure as deeply flawed as GAAP EPS, would you really expect them to wind up producing something better?

All is not bleak, however. Let's pick up the stories of Joel Stern, who documented the disconnect between EPS and valuation way back in 1974, and Amazon, the poster child for value creation without benefit of EPS. Stern went into the consulting business with another outstanding innovator in financial analysis. Bennett Stewart created an improved profit measured called economic value added (EVA).

One feature of Stewart's alternative approach was to put R&D and advertising expenditures on the company's balance sheet, rather than treating them as expenses that reduce income. Amazon measured up more favorably with EVA than in conventional securities analysis. That was because its comparatively narrow profit margins were offset by high turnover of its merchandise. In his 2013 book, *Best Practice EVA*,[9] Stewart wrote about what happened in the period after Amazon first reported positive annual earnings, according to GAAP.

Over a five-year span, Amazon's EPS plunged from a peak of $2.50 a share to −$0.33. During that time, the online retailer's margins collapsed, deeply negative cash flow from operations forced it to raise tons of new capital, and the company missed consensus EPS estimates for 11 consecutive quarters. The share price did exactly what you'd expect, given those facts. Well, no, actually. The price more than quadrupled, making AMZN one of the period's best-performing large-cap U.S. stocks.

Stewart recounted how the pundits offered a totally wrong explanation for this price response, which defied everything they'd previously said about how the equity market works. It wasn't that AMZN was a unique "story stock" driven by its visionary CEO Jeff Bezos, exempt from the forces that governed all other stocks' valuations. Instead, said Stewart, the investors who really matter looked through Amazon's GAAP earnings and focused instead on genuine economic profits.

Even as the company's EPS was spiraling downward, its EVA profits nearly tripled in the five years ending in mid-2013. AMZN's price went up and up as this happened, rather than down and down, as the doctrines tirelessly promoted by equity analysts and their enablers in the media said it had to. There could hardly be a more forceful demonstration that Joel Stern was correct way back in 1974, when he wrote that earnings per share don't matter for stock valuations.

Incidentally, those wiser-than-thou critics of Amazon in its pre-positive-EPS days were also wrong about the historical episode that's usually cited in connection with supposedly irrational overvaluations. "Tulip mania" refers to a seventeenth-century episode of speculation in the Netherlands. It's commonly stated, erroneously, that the prices of tulips rose to absurdly high levels. In fact, the activity involved certain rare varieties of tulip *bulbs*. Those, in fact, had great value for their ability to propagate, much as prize bulls are valued for their ability to sire many other prize bulls.

The economist Peter Garber long ago found that prices never got out of line for the rare bulbs capable of producing exceptionally beautiful flowers. Those specimens were traded by professionals in a well-organized exchange. The excesses occurred only in informal markets set up in taverns, where non-experts could take fliers on ordinary bulbs without having to back their speculations with significant amounts of cash.[10]

Garber's conclusions have been challenged by subsequent researchers. But what seems clear is that the history of the tulip mania isn't as clear-cut as maintained by the detractors of stock that pulls way, way out of the pack. So next time you hear a self-appointed guardian of market propriety invoke tulip mania to trash a high valuation on a zero-EPS stock, as if it proves that investors have taken leave of their senses, keep in mind that the celebrated pundit probably doesn't have a thorough understanding of the event.

Bottom Line on the Supposed Bottom Line

Let me summarize this exploration of the equity research community's favorite yardstick. EPS can't logically be the basis of how stocks get priced in the market. This isn't altered by the fact that it's arithmetically possible to divide a stock's price by its EPS to calculate a PE multiple, which can be compared with other companies' PE multiples. (I'll leave aside the conundrum of how to calculate a PE on a company that has negative EPS for the year.)

Even if EPS, rather than free cash flow, were the true source of a stock's value, using EPS to calculate the stock's proper price would be prone to error, due to accounting tricks that commonly render EPS misleading, if not fraudulent. Or if the reported numbers aren't fraudulent, they may be distorted by "accounting mistakes." And the erroneous EPS data may later be subject to a do-over. This is all in addition to EPS being based on accounting standards that don't apply very well to a large percentage of today's companies.

Wall Street research ignores these difficulties, blithely continuing to place EPS front and center. There's occasional talk of quality of earnings as a consideration in assigning PE multiples. Some research shops go as far as bringing more sophisticated financial theory into their reports. But the competition among analysts to be the best at what they do largely boils down to providing the most accurate forecast of a number that's frequently a work of fiction.

I recall once seeing a stock analyst at a leading Wall Street firm receive the news that his quarterly EPS estimate for one of his companies had matched the actual figure to the penny. He was punching the air and beaming like a baby boy with another brand-new choo-choo toy, to quote an antediluvian song lyric. This was a well-established expert in his field who seemingly had nothing left to prove. But I guess the thrill of nailing an artificially contrived number, long since shown to be irrelevant to stock valuation, never gets old.

The Guidance Game

Bennett Stewart's development of a superior profitability measure hasn't been just an academic exercise. Through his consulting work he has persuaded many corporations to adopt EVA as a management tool. For corporate executives using this tool, the objective is to maximize the wealth of the shareholders. That's certainly an improvement over managers maximizing their own wealth at the expense of shareholders.

In a perfect world, every corporation would shift its focus from EPS to a superior measure that truly advanced the objective of building shareholder wealth, be it EVA or another well-conceived yardstick. Stock analysts would then be compelled to redirect their efforts as well. Investors, in turn, would start to receive research reports that supplemented the analysts' valuable intelligence on companies' operations and prospects with genuinely helpful advice on valuation.

That would indeed be a perfect world. Here on earth, inertia controls much of what goes on in the business world. An immense infrastructure has been built up over many years on the foundation of predicting EPS, translating the predictions into price targets, debating the price targets in the media, and grading analysts and their firms on the accuracy of their predictions. Converting all the participants in this to a different, more complex metric wouldn't just be tantamount to moving a mountain. It would be more like moving a mountain range.

Refusing to conform to the established system could penalize a company in terms of the number of analysts following it. Wide analyst coverage is regarded as essential to obtaining a high stock valuation, and not necessarily without reason.

Omaima A.G. Hassan and Frank S. Skinner stated in a 2016 article that "it is well documented that analyst coverage affects firm value."[11] According to the previous research they cited, wide coverage makes it less costly for investors to monitor companies' activities. So owning the shares of widely covered companies is more profitable than owning stocks followed by only a few analysts.

One study concluded that analyst coverage makes companies' stocks more valuable by increasing the demand for their shares. This is true even when the analysts merely recycle existing facts instead of ferreting out new information. The SEC requires companies to report EPS anyway, so why not play along with the system, even if EPS has nothing to do with how management runs the business?

An essential part of playing along with the system is providing earnings guidance to analysts. This consists of management telling investors the level of EPS it expects to report for the current quarter and beyond. Guidance is carefully couched in language that allows the company to escape legal liability if the actual numbers turn out to be different.

A constructive view of earnings guidance is that it helps investors price stocks properly. After all, the share price is supposed to reflect a company's future performance, rather than earnings from past quarters that have already been reported in its financial statements. Who's in a better position to know how things are shaping up for the next few months than the company's own managers?

If investors were to rely solely on companies' guidance, analysts' EPS forecasts would become irrelevant. Fortunately for the analysts, investors continue to express interest in analysts' tweaks. For one thing, self-predictions by companies with earnings that are sensitive to the business cycle will depend on their internal outlooks on the economy. Analysts may get a better handle on key economic indicators with the help of their firms' economic teams.

Also, a corporation's managers spend a lot of effort building enthusiasm among the troops: "Rah! Rah! We're going to make that sales target. Yes!" They might find it difficult to switch hats in an instant to, "Here's a dispassionate view of what we're realistically likely to achieve." The managers' guidance might be biased to the optimistic side as a result.

Analysts who also cover the company's competitors will recognize the possibility that the companies' own earnings estimates may add up to more than the industry as a whole is likely to earn. It's mathematically impossible for every competitor to gain market share in the same period. So investors aren't crazy to suppose that analysts can be useful in tamping down excessive expectations built into guidance.

But any presumption that companies will invariably guide too much toward the upside doesn't fully account for how the guidance game is played. That's because there's a negative repercussion for a company that grossly overstates its expected EPS. Let me explain.

From the investors' perspective, the game's point is to determine whether the company is exceeding, meeting, or falling short of expectations. That's supposed to become clear when the company reports its actual EPS. Under the rules of the guidance game, a *beat*—exceeding the analysts' consensus by even one penny—means the company is outperforming expectations. When that happens, the stock is supposed to go up. A *miss*, on the other hand, indicates that previous expectations were too high. The stock has to follow the script and fall.

As I previously discussed, a company can employ various gimmicks to boost or restrain its reported EPS in any given quarter, so as to maintain a smooth upward path. Now imagine that all through the quarter, analysts are formulating a pretty accurate picture of how things are going at the company. They know what's happening on the ground through intelligence they've gathered from the company's suppliers, customers, and competitors.

The analysts' earnings estimates reflect all that information. But what the analysts don't know is that management is worried about reporting EPS that will be too high to exceed in next year's corresponding quarter. So management is planning to trim the quarterly number with some adroitly timed accounting adjustments.

When the company releases its artificially constructed EPS number, the analysts who've based their forecasts on the reality underlying the reported number wind up being much too high. Getting blindsided in this way makes the analysts look bad. Seeing that the company isn't playing by the rules, they may decide to stop following it in favor of another company that won't embarrass them. That's a bad outcome for the management that sprang the smoothing plans on the analysts at the last minute, since wider coverage is associated with better stock performance.

A better strategy is to guide analysts to a number close to the largely predetermined EPS figure. Not exactly to the number, mind you. The ideal outcome is for the analyst consensus to be at least $0.01 below the number that eventually gets reported. As *Barron's* put it in 2021, "Most companies tend to set expectations conservatively so that they can then exceed a low bar."[12]

This way, if everything goes as planned, the stock will rally on the EPS beat. By the rules of the game, nobody will fault analysts for being off by a penny or two. The analysts get credit for being able to forecast earnings with a high degree of accuracy. And even if the price spurt lasts for only a day, the stock builds a reputation as the kind you want to own. The message is, "The company's outstanding management team consistently exceeds expectations."

To paraphrase an old Wall Street joke, this cozy little system works out well for the companies, it works out well for the analysts, and two out of three ain't bad. The investors can't be said to benefit from an arrangement that discourages the sort of independent thinking that might just lead them to a hidden gem within the universe of stocks. But they're not the ones running this game.

Analysts operating within the established structure understand all too well the risks of ignoring company guidance. They can end up being right, according to the company's actual sales volumes and cost factors, but wrong, according to the EPS number concocted by management to avoid dreaded earnings volatility. From a career standpoint, the key thing is to avoid standing out with a way-off-the-mark forecast.

The safest strategy for analysts playing the guidance game is to stick close to the number being put out by management. After all, one of these quarters, business conditions may spoil the party. Actual revenues and costs might careen outside the range that management can control with channel-stuffing and discretionary accounting decisions. If that happens, analysts won't look any worse than their peers at other firms as long as they're close to the guidance-influenced consensus.

But what if an analyst thinks the price target implied by the prevailing group-think—otherwise known as the consensus—is unrealistically high? No problem. Just lower the stock's assumed PE multiple and presto, the price target is back to a realistic level.

In an extreme case, the incentives built into the Great Guidance Game could drive analysts all the way to perfect uniformity in their EPS forecasts. Once again, a bad outcome for investors. To the extent that analysts are focused on not looking bad in the guidance game, they're depriving investors of the benefit of their independent judgment.

Fortunately, the game doesn't normally work out that way. You can readily observe that analysts' estimates don't invariably converge exactly at the guidance number. But a 2020 incident provided evidence that analysts tend to avoid deviating too far from where the companies wish them to be.

At that time, the COVID-19 pandemic was creating major uncertainty about the economic outlook. In response, the *Wall Street Journal* reported, 180 of the companies in the S&P 500 stopped issuing guidance. With those helpful hints removed, the dispersion among analysts' earnings estimates became the widest since at least 2007.

Maybe dispersion would have increased in any event, given that the U.S. economy was in a recession in March–April 2020. But that recession was much milder than the Great Recession of 2008–2009. So if the divergence of estimates resulted primarily from economic contraction, it should have been greater in 2008–2009 than in 2020. We can conclude that to the extent that analysts' estimates bunch together, guidance does appear to play a role in it.

Making Nice to Management

One more reason for analysts to defer to companies' guidance is to preserve access to management. This includes obtaining face time for clients with companies' senior executives. Entrée at the corner office pays off.

A 2016 study by Ling Cen, Jing Chen, Sudipto Dasgupta, and Vanitha Ragunathan indicated that analysts who get invited to ask questions early during earnings calls have superior career trajectories.[13] And that sort of treatment by management isn't a random thing. According to a 2014 study by Lauren Cohen, Dong Lou, and Christopher J. Malloy, 59% of surveyed investor relations officers said that they actively manage the order in which analysts are called on to ask questions.[14]

A standing joke on Wall Street is about the frequency with which analysts suck up to corporate bigwigs with the phrase "Great quarter, guys!" The research firm Sentieo reported that in August 2021 mentions of those words and their synonyms set an all-time record of 327. "Congratulations" also made a strong showing, according to the financial website's analysis of earnings call transcripts.

In 2017 the *Wall Street Journal*'s Jason Zweig reported[15] on research by Jonathan Milian and Antoinette Smith.[16] They analyzed 16,000 earnings calls of 500 companies. Analysts on those calls described the quarterly results with the adjectives "good," "great," or "strong" more than 215,000 times.

Companies had good reason to encourage such obeisance. Milian and Smith calculated that the more lavishly analysts praised management's performance, the more the stock shot up after the earnings announcement. Zweig's description of analysts' behavior on earnings calls included the phrases "craven flattery," "lapdog," "snivel," and "bootlicking sycophants." Newsletter writer Marc Rubinstein's account[17] invoked "cozy up to management" and "public debasement in exchange for private access."

Perhaps these findings don't completely justify calling "Beat-the-Consensus" a rigged game. But consider the following statistics, reported in early 2022 by Reuters. Out of 180 companies that had reported 4Q 2021 earnings by that time "just" 78.8% had beaten analysts' consensus estimates, according to Refinitiv. According to the Reuters headline, Wall Street was underwhelmed by the latest results. Over the previous four quarters, by contrast, an average of 84% of earnings reports were beats.

Any odds maker whose lines on sporting events resulted in an 80% ratio of winning bets would go bust. The handicapper's goal is to set the line so that half the bettors win and half lose. If that happens the bookie—or legal gaming site, as the case may be—profits by raking in the vigorish, a fixed percentage of the amount wagered.

EPS forecasting isn't organized on the same business model. But a naïve investor who's familiar with the concept of an unbiased prediction probably assumes that when a company beats the consensus forecast, it genuinely represents a surpassing of previous expectations. That's simply not a valid conclusion when the vast majority of outcomes are beats.

Deviating from the Script

If you're feeling outrage at this point, let me add something to the story that may calm you down a bit. A system that involves management control over setting expectations, with full cooperation from the analysts, is a dandy arrangement from the companies' standpoint. But that's not how things always play out in practice. Analysts' EPS forecasts don't actually congregate right at the guidance number. Sometimes several analysts are well outside the pack, both above and below the consensus. What's "going wrong" in those instances?

The fact is that some companies simply don't fit very well into the EPS/PE/PT/Guidance ecosystem. Their revenues and, consequently, their profits are extremely hard to predict with any accuracy, even over a period as short as the next three months. These aren't companies that rely almost entirely on recurring revenue sources. They don't compete in industries in which market shares change only glacially from year to year. The ups and downs of their sales don't correlate with familiar economic indicators.

These companies' financial success depends on continuously coming up with new products that may or may not catch on in intensely competitive markets. They may operate in technologically dynamic industries, where the interval between revolutionary innovation and obsolescence is brief. Or the company's revenues may depend on generating entertainment content that has massive popular appeal. There's no way of knowing for certain what moviegoers or music fans will go for. And if a company with highly uncertain prospects manages to catch lightning in a bottle, there's no guarantee that it can do it again next year.

As we'll see when we study the #1 stocks in detail, this sort of unpredictability can be a virtue. Suppose a company has a valuation that reflects the consensus expectation, but it winds up exceeding the most optimistic, far-outside-the-pack analyst's assessment of its prospects. The company's stock will probably go up way more than the average stock. Its price may even double in the space of a year.

But there's another side to that coin. Precisely because the range of plausible outcomes is so wide for a company of this type, there's a substantial risk that its EPS will turn out to be worse than the most pessimistic analyst expects.

If that happens, the stock will probably finish closer to #500 than #1 in the S&P index.

Investors who get pulled into the EPS guidance game can receive a nasty surprise even with a company that has none of the characteristics I've just described. Note the phrase a few paragraphs back: "If everything goes as planned." An unplanned-for event such as a natural disaster, a strike, a calamitous industrial accident, or loss of a major customer can upset the otherwise steady revenue stream of a mature company in a low-tech, non-cyclical industry.

It won't matter that up until the moment the bad news crossed the screen, the analysts' EPS estimates were all bunched around the company's guidance. Through no fault of the analysts, none of their earnings models included the one factor that really mattered for the quarter. Theorists might be curious whether the PE multiples that the analysts applied to their EPS forecasts somehow incorporated the small risk of an event like the one that occurred. But as a practical matter, it's an all-around disaster, for the company, the analysts who follow it, and—no surprise here—the shareholders.

Potholes in the Road Paved with EPS

Here's another way you can get tripped up by linking your trades to the guidance game: Suppose you identify an analyst with a knack for anticipating a company's short-run zigs and zags. Over a period of several years, the company has beaten the consensus when this analyst's forecast has been above the consensus and missed when it's been below consensus. This time the ace's forecast is above consensus. The forecast is well supported by a current research report that meticulously analyzes all the important drivers of the company's earnings. You buy call options on the stock, expecting to make a quick profit and then wait to see how the analyst sizes up the next quarter.

Earnings come out and just as your hot-handed analyst predicted, the company beats by a few cents. But to your dismay, the stock goes down instead of up and your trade is a loser. As it turns out, EPS exceeded the consensus, but the company's gross margin fell short of expectations. In this particular quarter, the market cared more about the company's gross margin than about the usual center of attention, EPS.

In some other quarter, the stock may fall despite a beat on EPS because the company's updated guidance for the next quarter is lower than the market was looking for. Key takeaway: It's hazardous to participate in a game where the rules can change without warning.

An additional hazard can arise from following an analyst who isn't genuinely producing independent analysis. Let me hasten to say that I don't think that sort of slackness is typical. Most analysts, I believe, work extremely hard to give their stock-picking customers an edge. They do this even though they know that companies can pull the rug out from under them at any time with an arbitrary accounting adjustment. Although I think most stock analysts are on the up and up, an experience I once had on Wall Street taught me the importance of probing what's underlying an analyst's EPS forecast.

My firm's compliance department asked me to resolve a divergence in opinions about a particular company by the equity analyst and the corporate bond analyst assigned to it. To understand the problem, you have to be aware that, contrary to what some investors may suppose, bond analysts don't simply examine a company's balance sheet and calculate a credit-risk score based on measures such as the debt-to-equity ratio. Like their counterparts in stock research, they strive to be forward-looking.

One of the key future numbers that bond analysts try to get a handle on goes by the acronym EBITDA, which stands for earnings before interest, taxes, depreciation, and amortization. Earnings are generally the swing factor in projecting future EBITDA. That's because most of the other components are largely locked in from the outset of the year. In the case of taxes, the number is a highly predictable percentage of pretax earnings.

In the situation I was involved in, the bond analyst's projection of the coming year's earnings was considerably more pessimistic than his equity research counterpart's. The compliance department worried, not unreasonably, that if the stock wound up performing poorly, customers who lost money would sue. Their lawyers would argue that our firm knew the equity analyst's EPS forecast was unrealistic, as evidenced by our bond analyst's more conservative projection.

Incidentally, this scenario is less farfetched than it sounds to readers who aren't familiar with securities litigation. I once met a fellow alumnus of my college who had a dozen separate lawsuits going against brokerage firms with which he traded. Initially, I suspected—somewhat cynically, I admit—that his trading strategy was, "If the stock goes up, I win. If it goes down, I sue." But the guy seemed totally sincere in the belief that he'd been cheated in every single instance where his infallible judgment failed to produce a profit.

Getting back to the main story, we had to get the two analysts' earnings predictions better in sync to avoid potential legal liability. I figured this would be easy to accomplish. I obtained the bond analyst's spreadsheet for his earnings projection. It included estimates for each line of the company's income statement for the coming year—cost of goods sold; selling, general, and administrative expenses; and so forth. Then I phoned the stock analyst and asked him to provide his corresponding spreadsheet so that we could compare the two. We could then determine the source of the disagreement about the bottom line, that is, earnings.

After realizing that a couple of days had passed and I hadn't heard back from the stock analyst, I called again and he assured me he'd send his spreadsheet right over. Several days later, when it still hadn't arrived, it dawned on me that there wasn't any such document. The stock analyst's published report showed just a revenue forecast and an EPS forecast. He hadn't worked his way down from the top to the bottom of the company's income statement. Instead, he simply plugged in the company's revenue and earnings guidance, perhaps modifying it slightly to avoid being too obvious. It was certainly a more efficient, streamlined procedure than the hardworking bond analyst followed.

Rest assured, I don't believe this shortcut method is representative of most stock analysts' practices. But neither should you assume that analysts who grind away for countless hours are guaranteed to generate output that will help you create an index-beating portfolio. Even less assured is their ability to steer you toward the very best performing stock in the S&P 500.

No one expects perfect foresight from stock analysts. But at the very least, you might hope for a clear signal when things are starting to change direction. Your hopes for that modest benefit may remain unfulfilled. In July 2022, longtime market strategist Richard Bernstein commented[18] that

Wall Street analysts' outlooks are invariably positioned in the middle of a market cycle. "When you start getting 'negative surprises' in corporate earnings—when a lot of companies aren't meeting expectations—analysts will say at first that it's an aberration."

Later, according to the head of Richard Bernstein Advisors, the analysts will gang together and cut their forecasts sharply. Then, when things finally start to turn around, analysts will be slow to recognize it. "Nobody will want to be the first to say that, either," said Bernstein.

There's also a risk that an analyst's conclusions will be influenced, even if only subconsciously, by considerations that have nothing to do with recommending the best possible stocks. Sometimes an analyst's assigned industry falls out of favor. That situation may persist for years, unfortunately for the analyst's career ambitions or yearning for the limelight. It would be only human in the face of such a roadblock to convince oneself that the great mass of decision makers have it all wrong.

The resulting narrative is familiar: "These stocks are unjustly disfavored. The way to make money in the market is to buy what everybody hates." If it's too much of a stretch to make a case for the group, there's another route available. The analyst may try to convince investors that one stock within the group differs in some essential way from its competitors but "has been tarred with the same brush."

Or, "They've thrown out the baby with the bathwater." An even more colorful cliché goes, "When the police raid the brothel, they even arrest the piano player."

Could people with the grave responsibility of dispensing investment advice truly allow their judgment to be compromised by self-interest? I hope it won't shock you that the answer is yes. Let me share another anecdote.

I was once invited to be a panelist in a wide-ranging conference session. My assigned topic was speculative-grade debt, a category derogatorily referred to as "junk bonds." I assumed that what the program's sponsor wanted from me was to present a cogent analysis of the asset class's prevailing downside risks and upside potential, documented with concrete facts and figures. To the best of my ability, that's what I did in my allotted time. My 12-month outlook was for so-so returns on high-yield bonds—to call them by the purely descriptive name employed as far back as 1919.

Also on the panel were two equity portfolio managers. They interpreted the honor of being awarded a slot on the program quite differently. Both devoted their time exclusively to berating the audience for not being fully invested in stocks. Brushing aside signals suggesting that caution was warranted at that time, they cherry-picked some favorable indicators and delivered sermons on the virtues of equity investment. Never mind that the attendees had come to the conference to be enlightened rather than harangued.

The mission, as these panelists saw it, was to attract more capital to their asset class and, if possible, to their own organizations' billions of assets under management (AUM).

More AUM means more management fees, potentially leading to higher compensation for the portfolio managers. Do you suppose that motivation influenced their highly favorable assessment of the prospects for equities? And is it conceivable that the stocks on an analyst's coverage list, seen by most others as dead-in-the-water for the next couple of years, might appear attractive from the analyst's vantage point?

It Doesn't All Even Out in the End

Self-serving bias toward optimism isn't a potential problem only in out-of-favor industries. And it isn't just a potential problem, judging by data compiled by FactSet. In April 2022, John Butters from that company reported the following breakdown of thousands of analyst ratings on S&P 500 stocks, based on monthly averages over the preceding five years:

Buy	52.9%
Hold	41.1%
Sell	6.0%

This breakdown doesn't directly tell us how many of the S&P 500 companies are rated Buy, Hold, or Sell by a majority of the analysts following them. But it's mathematically impossible for every research organization represented in the survey to have an equal balance between Buy and Sell recommendations, yet produce so lopsided a mix of Buys and Sells in aggregate. We can therefore infer that the split between Buys and Sells within many research organizations tends to be closer to the nearly 9 to 1 ratio (52.9%/6.0%) shown above than to a 50/50 split.

That inference is supported by an analysis of recommendations issued by leading brokerage houses during August 2022. According to the MarketBeat data, the median ratio of Buys to Sells among the 18 firms was 7.1 times. The least unbalanced output among the 18 research departments was "only" 2.0 times as many Buys as Sells. At the opposite extreme, one brokerage house's mix included 60% Buys and 0% Sells, resulting in a ratio of infinity. The next-most-lopsided distribution was a 33 to 1 Buys-to-Sells ratio.

An overwhelming preponderance of Buys might seem to signal some sort of malfunction. Certainly, a dairy that set out to make equivalent amounts of chocolate and vanilla ice cream but instead produced 2 to 30 times as much chocolate as vanilla would reckon that something went wrong in the production process.

But consider the matter from the standpoint of an equity salesperson, whose compensation depends on generating lots of transactions. A Sell recommendation is useful only to customers who already own the stock. A Buy recommendation, on the other hand, is relevant to everybody on the salesperson's coverage list.

This includes customers who already own the stock. They might be talked into buying more when the analyst electrifies the market with the words "I'm reiterating my Buy." (That action might not satisfy finance professors' definition of "new information entering the market." But financial news editors are okay with reporters crediting a reiterated Buy for an otherwise unexplained price jump.) As far as the salesperson's bottom line is concerned, if analysts are working on reports that will culminate in Sell recommendations, they're not making the most productive use of their time.

Even if you aren't in the business of selling stocks, which makes a Buy report more useful to you than a Sell report, you too might see no problem with a 9 to 1 ratio between the two. After all, if the market as a whole rises by a significant amount, it's likely that many more stocks will go up than down. That will confirm that they were all good stocks to own at the time that the analysts made the recommendations. And the fact that the stock market dependably rises over the long run means that those trades will probably pay off sooner or later

The flaw in that reasoning is that equity analysts aren't paid to identify stocks that will go up at some point in the next several years, in line with a rise in the market as a whole. Investors who want to invest on that kind of premise buy index funds. There's nothing wrong with that, but equity research departments exist for the benefit of the other class of investors, the active managers who focus on security selection. They prefer the challenge of attempting to do better than the market average by picking stocks that will outperform.

Among the stock pickers are investment managers who are engaged in fierce competition for institutional assets. They face annual reviews by the pension plans and university endowments whose money they manage. Their performance is measured over quarterly, and even shorter, periods. One year of underperforming their benchmark (an index matched to the type of portfolio they run) probably won't cause clients to yank their money. But it steps up the pressure to outperform next time. Mutual fund managers' short-run results are out there for the world to see. If they want to run bigger funds and increase their personal compensation, they have to put up good numbers with a high level of consistency.

Since these managers' success is tied to market indexes, owning stocks that go up in a bull market isn't good enough. They need analysts to recommend stocks that will go up by more than the index when the market rises. Under this arrangement, a stock that goes down by less than the index in a bear market is actually a better recommendation than a stock that goes up by less than the index in a bull market. Recognizing that their professional customers' objective is to beat their benchmark, some research organizations use terminology along the lines of Outperform/Market Perform/Underperform, rather than Buy/Hold/Sell.

Now imagine you're a portfolio manager who's trying to excel within this set-up. The one indisputable fact you know is that by definition, half of the stocks in the index will do better than the median and half will do worse. Yet here you are, with your firm's most trusted research provider claiming that nine times as many stocks are going to beat the median as are going to return less than the median. Oh yes, that's in addition to assigning Hold ratings to about 40% of the stocks they cover. That rating implies that all those stock will match the index. That's one more thing that ain't gonna happen.

How can this research be useful to you when you know that its predicted outcomes are impossible?

Some market pros reading this will say that I don't understand how things actually work. Those Holds, they'll explain, are really Sells. If you count that way, the wildly skewed 52.9%/6.0% Buy/Sell ratio cited above magically turns into a 52.9%/47.1% Buy/Sell ratio. Not a perfect 50/50 split, but then again, neither is the proverbial coin flip. (Rigorous testing by Persi Diaconis, Susan Holmes, and Richard Montgomery found that 51% of the time, a coin will land on the side that was facing up when it was flipped.)[19]

"You see," the pros will continue informing me, "by taking the irresponsibly radical step of putting a Sell on a stock, an analyst would instantly become *persona non grata* with the company's management." No more front of the line to get picked to ask questions on earnings calls. No more open door at corporate headquarters for the analyst's VIP buy-side customers. A total freeze-out. Think Michael Corleone: "Fredo, you're nothing to me now. You're not a brother, you're not a friend. I don't want to know you or what you do."[20]

Fortunately, there's a way to avoid that terrible fate without losing all credibility by continuing to recommend an obviously overpriced stock. If the company's outlook is undeniably horrible, the analyst can lower the boom on it by downgrading it . . . all the way to Hold. This is done with a wink to those in the know. ("You understand, without my saying so, that this means 'Get out immediately,' right?") It's not exactly in line with the biblical injunction, make your yea a yea and your nay a nay. But it does get the point across and everybody saves face. What's the harm?

I get all that, but putting myself in the portfolio manager's shoes, I have some gnawing questions about this cozy arrangement. First of all, what's the difference between an actual Sell and a wink-wink Sell (otherwise known as a Hold)? Maybe Sell means, "Really, truly. I'm serious. Dump it right away!" Or maybe it just means, "Don't add to position." Am I supposed to exit the Holds but sell the Sells short, or what?

Also, you and I both know that nothing like 40% of the stocks in the index are going to perform close to the median. Within the S&P 500, the middle 40% by total return are those ranked 151 to 350. In 2021, the returns on those stocks ranged from 15.33% to 42.45%. That compared with a median (halfway between #250 and #251) of 28.17%. So some of those Holds validated their classifications as Sells in all but name, but others were stocks that would have helped me a lot in my quest to beat my benchmark. Does that mean, in reality, that some of those 200 stocks were "strong Holds" and some were "weak Holds"? Maybe in the future you could let me know which are which?

Based on the fact that some Holds massively outperform the averages, while others massively underperform, I'm inclined to agree with veteran traders who told me early in my career that there's no such thing as a Hold.

That designation is just a way for analysts to avoid taking a stance. Traders can't waffle; they have to hit the bid or lift the offer.

Finally, stepping back from all this, is the analyst's purpose to recommend good stocks to me? Or is it to avoid hurting the feelings of CEOs, whose multimillion-dollar compensation packages ought to constitute adequate cushions for such blows?

These objections, I hasten to say, haven't a prayer of changing the status quo. The established charade, in which "Hold" is code for "Sell," is too entrenched. On September 4, 2018, *Bloomberg News* reported that the mix of Wall Street analyst recommendations on Advanced Micro Devices was "balanced" at 14 Buys and 4 Sells. That 77.8%/22.2% ratio shifts to something in the vicinity of balanced, at 45.2%/54.8%, only if you count the 13 Holds as Sells.

It's reminiscent of a riddle, a version of which was reportedly used by Abraham Lincoln although he didn't originate it: How many legs does a dog have if you call his tail a leg? Answer: Four. Saying that a tail is a leg doesn't make it a leg.

Breaking Out of EPS/Guidance Prison

It's easy to get locked into an excessively narrow, EPS-obsessed view of the stock market. Quarterly earnings reports provide ready-made news events for the media. The quarterly ritual also gives analysts recurring opportunities to demonstrate their prowess as prognosticators. The hoopla surrounding these numbers fosters the illusion that equity returns are all about 90-day slices of a statistic that's been shown to play no part in how the market's real price-setters evaluate stocks.

Compounding the absurdity, the companies that are supposed to be measured by the master metric EPS have perfectly legal ways of altering it to their advantage. They also have some ability to constrain independent forecasts of the quarterly numbers by analysts, who risk looking bad if they stray too far from the companies' guidance. And by the way, some corporate players in the EPS game don't even focus on it for the internal process of running their businesses. But confronted with an elaborate structure erected on the foundation of EPS, investors fall into the trap. They conclude that their task is to anticipate beats and misses that will produce one-day price spurts or stumbles.

To the extent that investors look for a story to supplement this simplistic numerical analysis, the commentary they obtain from the media consists largely of uninformative sound bites. In many of those superficial discussions, the supposed rationale for buying this particular stock at this particular time involves something that was equally true last year and the year before that. ("Great company. Strong balance sheet. Seasoned management.") This unhelpful commentary typically comes from permabulls who act as advocates rather than analysts.

The saving grace is that confinement in EPS prison isn't a mandatory life sentence. It's eminently feasible to break out with the help of equity researchers who've caught up with Joel Stern's 1974 revelation that earnings per share don't count. Some have gone further, developing genuinely useful analysis for those willing to put in the effort to benefit from it.

To provide just a taste of what's out there, I looked over Bloomberg-compiled research reports of 2021 on Meta Platforms (FB), which was still known as Facebook at the time. I won't detail the methodology of every organization represented in that list. But I'm glad to say that there's legitimately useful information available for EPS escapees, even though in the end, some of the research departments still reduce their findings to EPS × PE = PT.

As I mentioned earlier, Stern highlighted free cash flow (FCF) as a more important determinant of stock prices than EPS. On a per share basis, FCF shows up as the numerator in a metric reported by Barclays, FCF yield. JPMorgan provides prospective FB buyers a variant it calls "FCFF yield."

Needham included in its summary a metric that labeled OIBDA (operating income before depreciation & amortization and stock compensation). PhillipCapital related its price target to its projection for discounted cash flow. That research provider stated that its price target also took into account qualitative factors such as the stock's risk-reward profile, market sentiment, the recent rate of share price appreciation, the presence or absence of stock price catalysts, speculative undertones surrounding the stock, and other factors. Note particularly the emphasis on catalysts. It contrasts with the less thoughtful form of value investing, which asks us to believe that one day the market will spontaneously recognize that the stock has been trading below its intrinsic worth for months or years.

The most thoroughgoing exit from the EPS × PE = PT paradigm among the FB reports is Valens Research's analysis. Valens stresses that its reports don't constitute Buy, Hold, or Sell recommendations on particular securities. The authors urge readers to consider other information in making their investment decisions. But Valens employs metrics of its own that probe more deeply than those found in most other research.

Providing detailed descriptions of all the Valens-devised valuation tools would make for extremely dense prose. But you can get the idea from one such tool. It consists of net working capital plus long-term non-depreciating operating assets. The latter component, in turn, includes land and non-depreciation operating intangible assets, excluding goodwill and other acquisition-related intangible assets.

As for the earnings calls that trigger-happy traders listen to for beats and misses, Valens applies a propriety process it calls "Earnings Call Forensics." This methodology examines and evaluates management's representations during the quarterly calls, as well as at other public events. Valens contends that broker-dealers are either unable or unwilling to use the techniques it employs, often out of fear of endangering their relationships with companies' management teams.

There's further good news for investors who harbor a suspicion that it's not in their financial interest to allow corporations, research departments, and the media to maneuver them into playing the guidance game. Some companies have opted out of providing guidance. Most conspicuously, perhaps, Berkshire Hathaway CEO Warren Buffett has said, "I think it's a very bad practice to be in the game of earnings guidance, and it is a game."[21] The Oracle of Omaha says he has seen guidance lead to a lot of bad things.

Hearteningly too, Berkshire forswears smoothing of its quarterly and annual results. In its "owner's manual," written by Buffett, the company colorfully vows that it will always tell shareholders how many strokes it took on each hole and will never play around with the scorecard. Reinforcing a key point of this chapter, Buffett points out that consolidated reported earnings may reveal relatively little about Berkshire's true economic performance, due to the limitations of conventional accounting.

In this context, Buffett sounds a lot like Joel Stern saying that the sophisticated investors who actually determine stock prices don't rely on accounting-based reported earnings. He expresses confidence that shareholders will fully realize the benefits of earnings that are unreportable under GAAP. The benefit will come through capital gains.

Finally, Berkshire rejects the "big bath" tactic employed by companies that suffer too big a loss to paper over with accounting sleight-of-hand. It's widely believed that while a big loss is bad for a stock, a bigger loss isn't worse for the stock. So if a quarterly loss from legitimate business setbacks is inevitable, that's a convenient time to take a whole bunch of write-offs. Management often has a backlog of write-offs that it had planned to postpone until they could be used to offset an unusual gain that it wouldn't be able to replicate in the corresponding quarter a year later.

Since management doesn't think another hundred million dollars of losses will do any more damage to the share price, why not take even bigger write-offs than necessary? This can be an opportune time to deal with a variety of items that management has purposely overlooked until now in order to avoid reporting anything but a steady climb in reported earnings. The balance sheet still assigns full value to some shaky debts, tired inventory, and goodwill arising from acquisitions that didn't pan out as hoped.

By being extra aggressive about writing down those assets, management can create a "cookie jar" of written-off assets. It can write them back up when—surprise!—the previous accounting treatment turned out to be too conservative. And wouldn't it be a stroke of good luck if that revelation just happened to occur during a quarter in which weak earnings were otherwise threatening to spoil the company's smooth upward progression?

Final Thoughts on Fundamental Analysis

The ultimate point of this extended tour of equity analysts' methods is not to dispute that they sometimes generate extremely profitable stock recommendations. One extraordinary example occurred in August 2022. A London-based Jefferies analyst, Charles Brennan, predicted in a note to investors that a wave of takeovers in the European tech sector would continue. He helpfully included a diagram of acquirers' possible targets.

The very next evening, the Canadian software company Open Text Corp. announced that it would acquire Micro Focus International. Brennan had identified the UK enterprise software developer as the second-most-likely takeover target on his list. Open Text's bid represented a 99% premium over the previous close. When Micro Focus International reopened for trading, the price zoomed almost to that level. Holders nearly doubled their money in the space of about 24 hours.

If this kind of thing happened every day, an investor really could start with a small grubstake and make enough money in the space of a year to retire for life. But as I stress throughout this book, that isn't a realistic or appropriate aspiration. Patience is an indispensable component of a successful investor's psyche.

There are two valid reasons to try to pick next year's #1 stock, if that excites you. The first is that it can provide an outlet for the speculative urge that won't harm you financially if you allocate just a percent or two of your portfolio to your annual pick. The second is that conducting the research needed to make your selection can teach you valuable things about the dynamics of stock prices. Those lessons will help you assemble a well-chosen, responsible equity portfolio.

What you should take away from the preceding overview of fundamental equity research is that the analysis published by brokerage houses and independent research firms, useful though it may be in other respects, isn't geared to the specific objective of identifying in advance the single best-performing stock in the S&P 500. Those organizations are rewarded if they enable managers of diversified portfolios to beat their investment benchmarks by modest margins and avoid large losses. Looking for #1 requires an entirely different focus.

As for Technical Analysis . . .

The opening section of this chapter mentioned that equity analysts' study of a company's fundamentals—competitiveness, financial strength, earnings, and so on—is supplemented by the work of technical analysts who focus instead on a stock's price behavior. They construct charts of the stock's past price movements, believing that certain observable patterns provide useful indications of its future price. Many stock pickers take both fundamental and technical conclusions into account.

A comprehensive assessment of technical analysis is a great topic for another author, time, and place. The purpose of this book is to assist in the effort to identify in advance the year's best-performing stock. Toward that end, I'll just provide some reasons to doubt that technical analysis provides a quick, easy solution to that puzzle.

In my role as book review editor of the *Financial Analysts Journal* I reviewed a 2009 book by Andrew W. Lo and Jasmina Hasanhodzic titled *The Heretics of Finance: Conversations with Leading Practitioners of Technical Analysis.*[22] It's a serious, methodologically rigorous book that's by no means unsympathetic to the chartists' efforts to generate useful investment advice by studying price histories.

In fact, the authors summarize a study that found 10 price patterns favored by technical analysts to be statistically valid. They stop short of inferring from these findings that technical analysis can lead to profitable trading strategies. Still, they urge finance professors, who are generally skeptical about technical analysis, to open a dialogue with its practitioners.

Lo and Hasanhodzic's open-mindedness on the subject contrasts with the conviction of hardcore believers in efficient markets that a stock's past price movements have no bearing whatsoever on its future price movements. According to that view, a stock's price changes because new information arrives that alters the stock's intrinsic value. End of story. To efficient market hardliners, the countless hours that technical analysts spend on predicting future stock prices is at best a total waste of time.

The technical analysts interviewed in *The Heretics of Finance* don't exactly counter this criticism with concrete evidence that their labors meet high scientific standards. Here's a sample of their responses to the suggestion that their work ought to pass the test of empirical verification:

- "I doubt that many of the theories have been—or can be—back-tested."
- "Few things in life are perfectly black or white."
- "Technical analysis is an art."

If those comments don't inspire confidence, consider how Lo and Hasanhodzic's interviewees answered the question "Do you think that the inclusion of astrology in technical analysis undermines the credibility of the craft?" Their replies include the following:

- "Could astrology in some offhand way be beneficial or instructive? I'm going to say yes."
- "It depends on the type of astrology you're talking about."
- "I've seen some people make some very good calls using astrology."
- "Astrology is bad for technical analysis only in the eyes of closed minds."

Skepticism about the usefulness of technical analysis isn't restricted to academics. The renowned market analyst Laszlo Birinyi tells Lo and Hasanhodzic that the discipline is problematic due to an absence of hard and fast rules and proven theories. "It allows you to pick a stand and then find things that support your stand," he says. Birinyi has debunked some venerable technical rules and flatly declares, "The truth is technical analysis doesn't work in the market." He notes that anybody who relied on the chartists' cherished advance/decline ratio would have stayed out of stocks all the way from 1957 to 2002.

Unfazed by outright dismissals of their work, the technicians insist that theirs is the true path to stock market enlightenment. Robert Prechter scoffs at the notion of deepening the insights of technical analysis by combining it with fundamental analysis. In his opinion, that's like asking, "Is food more effective when used on its own or when combined with arsenic?" Confronted with the criticism that charting is inherently backward-looking, Alan Shaw counters that fundamental analysts are also backward-looking in their reliance on income statements and balance sheets. This skips over the fact, emphasized throughout the preceding critique of the fundamental approach, that analysts' price targets are based on *projected* EPS.

Technical analysis has legions of fans, but its detractors seem to be more outspoken than critics of fundamental analysis. Without specifying "technical" or "fundamental," I searched Google for the phrase "Is stock analysis bogus?" The first batch of headlines included the following:

- "Why Technical Analysis Is Useless"—Seeking Alpha
- "Is it proven that technical analysis of stocks is a fraud?"—Quora
- "Why Technical Analysis is Nonsense"—Seeking Alpha
- "Technical Analysis Is Fundamentally Flawed"—forbes.com
- "Is Technical Analysis Bogus?"—Mitchell Rosenthal, medium.com

That last headline is for an article that's actually constructive on technical analysis. But it's revealing that the author sees a need to answer the question he poses. There were no comparably deprecating comments or pointed questions about fundamental analysis among the top hits generated by asking if that approach is bogus. As extensively documented in this chapter, fundamental securities analysis isn't immune from criticism. But only technical analysis, whether fairly or otherwise, generates the intense skepticism that a quick search of the Internet produces.

It's faint consolation for technicians that their image has improved from "low-level criminals." That's how they were perceived in the 1920s, according to technical analyst Anthony Tabell. In those days, *point-and-figure charts* were used in apparent attempts to benefit from pools. Those were collusive efforts to manipulate stocks, which were disreputable although not yet illegal at the time. Tabell said that cloud continued to hang over technical analysts' reputation as late as the 1950s.

The purpose here, however, is neither to bury technical analysis nor to praise it. What matters to this book's theme is what can help investors who want to take a shot at picking the #1 stock. That's not the specific focus of technical analysts. Neither is that the goal of their fundamental counterparts who make EPS forecasts, apply PE ratios, and generate price targets. Whatever the merits of their respective disciplines may be, stock pickers who are trying to zero in on the coming year's biggest gainer must look beyond their input. One logical place to look is in the stories of the stocks that have captured that crown in the past. Let's now turn to that topic.

Chapter Two

These Are Their Stories

~

THE PREVIOUS CHAPTER SHOWED why you probably won't find next year's #1 S&P 500 stock by relying solely on standard equity research. Analysts slap Buy recommendations on about half of all stocks, but only one can be #1, as measured by total return. To narrow the field down, you have to look for some additional qualities that can't be reduced to numbers. One good way to pick up some clues is to study the stories of stocks that topped the list in the past. No two years are exactly alike, but this process will identify factors that cut across all years.

For each #1 stock from 2017 to 2021 I've pulled together stories you haven't read anywhere else. Sure, you may have seen or heard some comments here and there about stocks that really broke out of the pack in one year or another. But because no one knew which stock was going to end up #1, no journalist started focusing on that stock before it began its run, with the objective of figuring out why it was set up to succeed so sensationally.

The significance of many events that contributed to these stocks' spectacular gains became apparent only after the fact. And some of the stocks that wound up being the #1 for the year got off to a slow start. As a result, they weren't necessarily the ones getting the most attention.

There's just one way to get a full account of a stock's championship year. Somebody has to piece it together from all the daily news reports about the company, in both the year before and the year of its triumph.

That somebody turned out to be me. The results of my detective work make up the rest of this chapter. In a later one I'll distill the common characteristics from these stories. Those are the traits to look for in your search for the next #1.

2017: NRG Energy (NRG) 134%

On December 31, 2015, *Bloomberg* identified NRG as the S&P 500's third-most-underpriced stock, compared with the average of analysts' price targets. The electric utility's shares were trading 70% below that benchmark. This insight wasn't much of a help over the next 12 months, as NRG produced a total return of 6%, way below the S&P 500's 12%. Even more discouragingly, NRG badly underperformed its peer group, as the utilities subindex returned 16%.

Analysts felt confident that NRG had the financial moxie to grow into their price targets because of its strong balance sheet in an industry known for heavy reliance on borrowed money. The parent company had no debt coming due until 2018, plus plenty of cash. Over half of its available bank credit was undrawn.

In short, analysts saw vast unrealized potential in NRG a full year before its 2017 breakout, when it outpaced all other stocks in the S&P 500. And it wasn't a matter of investors suddenly waking up one day and realizing NRG was undervalued. ("How could we have been so blind until now?") That's the caricature of actual stock market behavior that some hypesters present in touting their picks. In the real world, something has to change for a stock's unrealized potential to be unlocked. A fancier way of saying is that it requires a *catalyst*. So let's see what was holding NRG back during 2016 and what it was that changed the dynamics in 2017.

Heading into 2016, NRG shareholders were restless. The stock stood at half its price of 10 years earlier, and it was the utilities subindex's worst performer in both 2014 and 2015. Many investors blamed the stock's languishing on CEO David Crane's vision of transforming NRG from a major player in generating electricity from fossil fuels to a leader in renewable energy. It was a public-spirited ambition, but the winds of change were blowing at NRG. In December 2015 the Board fired Crane. Afterwards, the deposed CEO said that he'd wanted to expand in the exciting field of green energy, while retaining the company's coal-fired plants, but investors' preference for safe, steady returns won out.

NRG kept talking the talk on the transition to the new era of renewables, but the company was now set on a different path. Wind and solar accounted for less than 10% of NRG's power generation, but the Board was reportedly disgruntled over the performance of NRG's residential solar unit. That business was scaled back during the year. In March 2016, the company cut its dividend, giving it greater flexibility to commit capital to the areas that would now be emphasized.

Wall Street continued to see huge unrealized potential in NRG. By October the stock had moved from third to first place within the S&P 500 in undervaluation, relative to analysts' average price target. In November Lawrence Strauss of *Barron's* named NRG as one of the market's best utility plays. Deutsche Bank analyst Abe Azar said the only thing holding the stock back was a need to negotiate a debt reduction at GenOn Energy, a wholly owned subsidiary acquired in 2012.

As an indication of GenOn's dire financial straits Standard & Poor's downgraded the company in January 2017 from CCC to CCC−, just three notches up from D for default. For good measure, the rating agency said GenOn's rating was likely to head even lower. S&P warned that GenOn had no credible plan for addressing debt soon coming due, heightening the risk of bankruptcy by June.

One week after the GenOn downgrade, a catalyst for NRG to realize its potential appeared in the form of some activist investors. Elliott Associates and affiliated companies, with combined economic exposure equivalent to 6.9% of NRG's shares, formed a pact with Bluescape Energy Partners and an affiliate with a 9.4% aggregate economic exposure. The two organizations said they'd soon begin talks with NRG's Board and were evaluating the possibility of nominating one or more directors.

Elliott, founded by Paul Singer, had previously played a leading role in efforts to unlock value at companies such as Hess Corporation, Mentor Graphics, PulteGroup (the #1 S&P 500 stock of 2012), and Telecom Italia. Bluescape was headed by C. John Wilder, the former cost-chopping CEO of TXU (later Energy Future Holdings), described as a "turnaround titan" by *Bloomberg News*. Shortly after these heavyweights disclosed their involvement in NRG, BlackRock, the world's largest asset manager, disclosed that its constituent firms had increased their NRG stake to 6.5%.

The prospect of some shaking up by activists had an immediate impact. NRG jumped by 35% in January 2017, by far the biggest gain among utilities. CNBC's Jon Najarian said the stock was up on speculation that the company had hired an advisor in connection with a takeover at a price in the $20s. NRG had begun the month at $12.26.

With powerful players agitating for NRG to change its ways, David Crane's successor as CEO, Mauricio Gutierrez, made it clear that a revised company profile was in the works. The days of the pure independent power producer were over, he stated. And NRG was already making the sort of cost cuts called for by the activists.

In February NRG announced an agreement with Elliott and Bluescape. The company formed a business review committee to study operating and cost-cutting initiatives, along with potential additions to or subtractions from NRG's collection of businesses. Bluescape's Wilder and the former chairman of the Texas public utility commission joined the Board, replacing the company's nonexecutive chairman and one other incumbent director. As part of the deal, the two activist investors agreed not to increase their NRG holdings for the time being.

Meanwhile, time was running out on GenOn's need to deal with its soon-to-mature debt. NRG wasn't responsible for paying that debt, but it represented a stain on NRG's otherwise clean corporate-wide bill of financial health. NRG didn't need that kind of dampener of investor enthusiasm, particularly at the same time as it was reporting disappointing first-quarter earnings. After a stretch of exceeding analysts' forecasts, NRG fell short of the lowest of all their estimates.

A breakthrough occurred on May 4 as GenOn announced a proposed note offering. Together with cash on hand, said the company, the deal's proceeds would suffice to repay the debt coming due the following month. The possibility of a near-term bankruptcy would be averted. NRG shares jumped 11% on the news.

Later that month GenOn reached an agreement with NRG and its noteholders to reorganize its capital structure through a bankruptcy filing. Holders of the notes due in June received cash to the tune of 92% of their principal. NRG's stock rose on the news.

While the GenOn debt millstone was being eliminated, NRG's business review committee was reportedly considering a recommendation to sell off the company's renewables operations. Prospective buyers had informally expressed interest in buying the whole kit and caboodle. Numerous climate-conscious pension funds and insurance companies lurked in the wings as potential acquirers.

On July 12 the committee announced a $1.1 billion cost reduction plan involving both job cuts and asset sales. With cash raised from asset sales, NRG planned to retire debt and possibly pay special dividends. NRG stock responded with a one-day gain of 29%, bringing its year-to-date advance to 72%. Pleased with the results of its activism, Elliott took profits on one-third of its NRG holdings.

NRG did in fact redeem two of its outstanding debt issues before the year was out. In recognition of the further balance sheet improvement, Moody's raised the outlook on its rating from Stable to Positive. In conjunction with its third-quarter earnings release, NRG announced a 3% dividend increase.

In summary, the more than doubling of NRG's price in 2017 didn't result from the scales suddenly falling from investors' eyes. Analysts had identified vast unrealized price potential a year or more earlier. But transforming that potential into reality required the prodding of two big league activist investors to persuade management to chart a new course more to the investment community's liking. Resolution of a subsidiary's looming debt crisis was another essential ingredient.

NRG's change of direction wasn't designed to please activists of a different sort. Clean energy advocates presumably would have preferred the company to push further into that business rather than reverse course. Fortunately, from the green camp's viewpoint, the review committee's plan called for selling rather than shutting down the renewables businesses. There was no shortage of candidates to take over their operation. One lesson to draw from NRG's story is that a company is more likely to get its stock to #1 by delivering what the market wants at a given time than by convincing the market that it's looking for the wrong thing.

2018: Advanced Micro Devices (AMD) 80%

If you try to figure out why a semiconductor manufacturer such as Advanced Micro Devices does well or poorly in a given period, you'll quickly encounter a daunting mass of dense technical jargon. Many different types of chips serve a wide variety of uses. The field evolves so rapidly that one article published in 2018 derided an ancient technology introduced way back in 2014. And it's not as if the experts who devote their lives to studying this industry unanimously agree about which company's current chip provides the biggest bang for the buck. Or, more important, which still-in-development, next-generation chip will dominate in the period ahead.

Before you conclude that to understand the chip business you'll have to obtain a degree in electronics engineering (assuming you don't already have one), take heart. Less technically arcane factors explain why AMD finished dead last in the Philadelphia Stock Exchange Semiconductor Index (SOX) in 2017—making it that year's only decliner in the group—yet topped not only its chip-making peers but the entire S&P 500 the very next year. It boiled down to the competitive struggle, particularly among Advanced Micro, Intel, and Nvidia. As Barclays Capital analyst Blayne Curtis has put it, "Investing in these chip companies is all about believing that their technology is better than the competition."

Certainly, there were other influences on AMD's stock price. One positive factor was a strengthening in the company's financial position. Over the course of 2017–2018, AMD was jostled as semiconductor stocks, and more broadly the tech sector, went into and out of favor. Also playing a role were the waxing and waning fortunes of cryptocurrencies. Crypto-miners had become major consumers of semiconductors.

Something else that mattered was the political backdrop. The Trump administration was considering a tightening of trade restrictions with China, where many of the chips marketed by U.S. semiconductor companies were manufactured. But notwithstanding those powerful, industry-wide forces, Advanced Micro's prospects heading into 2018 depended heavily on company-specific factors.

The company was undergoing a transition. It was previously known mainly for producing commodity chips for personal computers. Now Advanced Micro was making a push into higher-performance—and higher-margin—chips in areas such as the graphics processing unit (GPU) market for data centers and deep-learning computing for the automotive market, which was moving toward self-driving vehicles.

There appeared to be huge potential in this redirection. Canaccord Genuity analyst Matthew Ramsay estimated that the changes could double the profit margins Advanced Micro had been generating with its established product line. But judging by AMD's 2017 performance, the market wasn't yet convinced that the potential would be realized. Its −9% return compared with 22% for the S&P 500.

Before 2018 began, some key elements were already in place for a big rebound. For one thing, rating upgrades by Moody's and Standard & Poor's during 2017 attested to Advanced Micro's improving credit profile. Also, there was a big opportunity for the company to grab market share in servers. Leading cloud service operators such as Alphabet, Amazon, and Microsoft wanted an alternative to Intel, which overwhelmingly dominated the market.

In addition, Advanced Micro's graphics cards, which were used in mining cryptocurrencies, got a shot in the arm when crypto prices soared, making mining much more profitable. The company's graphics line scored a big design

win at Amazon Web Services. Advanced Micro scored
again in the fast-growing artificial intelligence segment as
Tesla decided to reduce its reliance on Nvidia. On top of
all this, AMD looked cheap, based on recent multiples paid
by acquirers of semiconductor companies, as detailed by
Jefferies analyst Mark Lipacis.

Despite all these indications of substantial upside,
a series of setbacks tanked AMD's price in 2017. January
brought an unfavorable report on shipments of personal
computers, a key market for Advanced Micro. In March,
a review in a trade publication criticized a new Advanced
Micro chip's performance in video gaming. Goldman Sachs
initiated coverage of AMD in April with a Sell recommendation, noting that price cuts by Intel and Nvidia had
thwarted the company's past attempts to capture market
share through technological advances. As for the crypto
boom, it might quickly turn to crypto bust, so sales to that
market were inherently volatile. JPMorgan Chase CEO
Jamie Dimon didn't help on this score when his denuncia-
tion of cryptocurrency as a fraud attracted wide attention.
Finally, analysts pointed out that any financial benefits from
Advanced Micro's Tesla deal were off in the distant future.

So there were plenty of reasons for AMD holders to be
discouraged during 2017. But if anything, the stock's under-
performance made it look more attractive to its believers.
At year-end, BofA Merrill Lynch included AMD among its

10 best ideas for the first quarter of 2018. And with the new year, the company's fortunes immediately took a sharp turn for the better.

On January 3 AMD rose in response to a report claiming that Intel's chips contained a flaw that made the popular operating systems that employed them vulnerable to hackers. Patches that would be required for the Apple and Microsoft systems might slow down older machines operating on them. Later in the month *Barron's* backed up Intel's statement that its chips weren't actually flawed but worked as designed. Even properly functioning chips can be vulnerable to attack, the company pointed out. Even so, AMD gained 34% in January versus a "mere" 6% rise for the S&P 500.

As the year progressed, AMD rose on takeover speculation, as well as one of the more unusual bullish theses advanced in 2018 or possibly any other year. Jefferies analyst Mark Lipacis, already mentioned in this chronicle, highlighted the pending release of the movie *Ready Player One*, directed by Steven Spielberg. All the characters in that film live in, or escape to, a virtual reality world. If the movie hit it big at the box office, Lipacis theorized, it could stoke demand for virtual reality headsets. Those devices required high-performance GPUs manufactured by Advanced Micro and Nvidia. On a more mundane level, Advanced Micro's improving credit profile received further recognition through additional rating upgrades by Moody's and Standard & Poor's.

In June AMD again rose on the further misfortunes of its rival Intel, which delayed the release of a more advanced manufacturing process until sometime in 2019. That gave Advanced Micro a shot at gaining an edge in the high-performance personal computer and data center markets. At the same time, Advanced Micro was positioned for possible market share gains in lower-end graphics processing units and central processing units. Personal computer makers were looking for some relief from high component costs, and the relevant Advanced Micro chips were cheaper than Intel and Nvidia's, if not necessarily comparable in performance.

Not only were Advanced Micro's prospects looking bright, but its current financial performance was ringing the bell. Second-quarter earnings hit a seven-year high, putting a squeeze on the AMD bears. TheStreet called AMD "one of the hottest stocks on the planet." The shares jumped by 37% in August on further problems at Intel. On September 4, analyst Lipacis proclaimed that possibly for the first time ever, AMD was going to "ship a server microprocessor unit with higher transistor density than Intel." Ten days later, AMD hit its 2017 peak, up by 218% for the year.

The gain amassed by that point enabled AMD to capture the S&P's #1 spot for full-year 2017 despite losing 44%

of its value over the remainder of the year. The decline had several sources. Cryptocurrency prices plummeted and with them, the profitability of employing graphics processing units for crypto-mining. Intel reportedly overcame manufacturing problems that had been preventing it from keeping up with demand. On top of all that, the tech sector stumbled badly, with the S&P 500's information technology subindex shedding 18% of its value in the fourth quarter.

But as always, AMD was a beacon of hope for many. Some analysts urged investors to buy AMD on the dip, before it had a chance of once more wowing the market with the launch of its next-generation chip. Cowen analyst Matthew Ramsay called AMD his best idea for 2019. Even after an 80% advance in 2018, the AMD faithful were still enthralled.

2019: Advanced Micro Devices (AMD) 148%

Yep, that's right. Advanced Micro Devices was the #1 stock in the S&P 500 in both 2018 and 2019. It didn't do badly in 2020, either, finishing #7 with nearly a doubling (+99.98%). Something special was clearly going on with this semiconductor producer. And it wasn't a takeoff by a young company, producing spectacular growth that no mature company could hope to match. Advanced Micro celebrated its 50th anniversary in business during 2019.

Many of the same forces that alternately propelled and stifled AMD in 2018 drove the share price once again in 2019. Sector performance was a consistently favorable factor. The Philadelphia Stock Exchange Semiconductor Index rose quarter by quarter, finishing 33% higher for the year. Less steady and less prominent in 2019's play-by-play commentary on AMD was the trend of cryptocurrency prices. Bitcoin tripled in the first quarter, then gave back a big portion of its gains, netting out to a 75% rise on the year.

But the most important element of AMD's sensational rise in 2019 was the success of its new products. TheStreet's Scott Van Voorhis highlighted the company's growing momentum in the server market, its emerging technological edge in central processing units (CPUs), and its increasing competitiveness in graphics processing units (GPUs). Jefferies's Mark Lipacis reported that his checks of industry sources indicated a potential for Advanced Micro to gain significant market share in personal computers and data centers.

In May AMD took the year-to-date lead among all S&P 500 stocks as Cowen said the company's newest desktop and server CPUs "stole the show" at a trade show in Taipei, Taiwan. Standard & Poor's reaffirmed Advanced

Micro's improving credit picture with another rating upgrade. The credit agency said the company's strong product pipeline would facilitate additional market share gains in CPUs and enable further reductions in financial leverage.

In mid-March AMD jumped on the report of a major design win on Google's streaming-videogame service. Analysts found the one-day gain of 12% puzzling, as the report didn't truly represent fresh information entering the market. Advanced Micro's CEO Lisa Su had said at a January trade show that the company's GPU would be part of Google's new gaming project. She made the same point during an earnings call a few weeks later.

Perhaps it was a case of investors jumping on the bandwagon. Before the Google "news" arrived, AMD was up by 26% from its 2018 year-end level, double the S&P 500's 13% gain over the period. In that kind of environment, anything that even sounded like good news was another reason to buy. Investors who took time to investigate whether it genuinely represented something that wasn't previously known risked missing out on a further rise.

By the way, investors saw CEO Su as an essential ingredient in Advanced Micro's accelerating business success. Bloomberg's Pimm Fox had to qualify his finding that stocks of companies with female CEOs had outperformed those of companies with male CEOs, 20.7% to 8.5%. Su-led AMD's

175% gain during his measurement period skewed the statistics. In early August AMD sagged after the tech blog *Wccftech* claimed that Su was considering a jump to the #2 slot at IBM. The shares rebounded when she said there was "zero truth" to the report.

Advanced Micro continued to rack up business triumphs. AMD rose when the company inked a multi-year strategic partnership with Samsung. Under the agreement, the electronics giant would pay licensing fees and royalties for use of Advanced Micro's graphics technology in developing ultralow-power, high-performance mobile graphics intellectual property. AMD surged again on news that the company would be the main chip supplier for an upcoming Microsoft videogame console. Advanced Micro also announced partnerships with two leading producers of blockchain technology.

Susquehanna Financial Group analyst Christopher Rolland reported that based on his firm's retailer survey of more than 2,000 desktop personal computer configurations, Advanced Micro's market share in desktops was 20% as of the third quarter. That was up from 19% in the second quarter and 17% in 2018. Jefferies's Mark Lipacis enthused that the company was delivering on its promise to take share, as evidenced by a 50% quarter-over-quarter gain in servers versus 28% for Intel. As in 2018, Advanced Micro capitalized on a setback at Intel. Wells Fargo said, based on industry checks and a report by the website *SemiAccurate*, that Intel might be facing further delays of its 10-nanometer Lake Xeon Scalable Processor.

A nanometer is one-billionth of a meter. To give you some idea of how tiny that is, a sheet of paper is 100,000 nanometers thick. A nanometer is how much your fingernails grow in one second. Nanometers are prominent in semiconductor circles because manufacturing processes that lead to smaller-nanometer chips have traditionally resulted in faster and more power-efficient chips. AMD introduced a 7-nanometer chip that was taking share from Intel's mainly 14-nanometer chips, according to Susquehanna analyst Rolland.

One final development that ultimately helped make AMD the #1 S&P 500 stock of 2019 involved U.S.–China trade relations, which had been a drag on semiconductor stocks in 2018. This factor had remained a negative for most of 2019. AMD dipped in late June when the U.S. Commerce Department's Bureau of Industry and Security added the company's joint venture partner to its blacklist of companies that it deemed to be acting contrary to U.S. national security or foreign policy. Wedbush analyst Daniel Ives called mounting U.S.–China trade tensions "a black cloud across the tech space." But in December,

President Donald Trump tweeted that a Phase 1 U.S. trade deal with China was "VERY close." AMD gained on the news, along with shares of Micron Technology and Taiwan Semiconductor.

2020: Tesla (TSLA) 743%

Tesla ranks #1 among the five #1 S&P 500 stocks-of-the-year that this chapter studies in detail. In 2020 its shares rose by an astounding 743%. Note that in Tesla's case, percentage price gain was identical to total return because the electric vehicle (EV) maker wasn't paying a dividend at the time.

To put TSLA's percentage increase in perspective, it took the S&P 500 index 26-plus years to achieve a 745% gain, based on its year-end 2021 level of 4766.18 and measuring from 563.84 on September 1, 1995. TSLA made an essentially equivalent advance in just 12 months. That's not merely beating the averages. It's beating the living daylights out of them.

I got in on this astounding gain, although a bit early, thanks to a personal connection with a professor of innovation and technology at INSEAD. Michaël Bikard's research doesn't involve making stock recommendations. But he mentioned to me that Tesla almost uniquely ticked all the boxes that researchers in his field had identified as characteristics of ultimately successful enterprises. The case for expecting Tesla to prevail in its intensely competitive market consisted of the following points, as of 2018:

1. The architecture of Tesla's vehicles differs from anything that preceded it. It's extremely difficult for incumbent companies to replicate new architectures.
2. From the customers' perspective, Tesla's technology is clearly superior to anything that preceded it.
3. Hiccups during scale-up are unavoidable. But they may also create better buying opportunities for the stock.
4. Self-driving cars are coming soon. The most important source of competitive advantage for them is not technology but data.
5. Who has the most data? Tesla. By a very, very wide margin. Tesla should therefore dominate the self-driving car industry.

These characteristics all applied when I acquired my Tesla shares in December 2018. Professor Bikard had placed a five-year time frame on his thesis. I therefore continued to hold the stock, which paid off royally with the sensational 2020 advance.

But before that happened, TSLA fell short of the S&P 500's 31% return in 2019, clocking in at "only" 26%. TSLA wasn't yet an S&P 500 stock. In fact, it didn't get included until late in 2020, just in time to claim the title as the index's best performer.

Tesla still had a lot of baggage going into its miraculous year. Its losses in 2019's first two quarters followed assurances by CEO Elon Musk that the company's previous climb to profitability would be sustained.

On November 21, 2019, Musk attempted to dazzle the market by unveiling Tesla's newest product, a pickup he dubbed the "Cybertruck." Musk said the vehicle's superstrong steel could survive blows from a sledgehammer without denting. He added that the vehicle had hard-to-break armor glass.

Unfortunately, an on-stage demonstration went badly. Two throws of a metal ball left the truck's side windows badly damaged. "Oh, my f---ing god!" exclaimed Musk. "Well, maybe that was a little too hard." Fortunately, that misfire didn't dampen consumers' enthusiasm for the Cybertruck. A few weeks later Musk tweeted that Tesla had received 250,000 preorders.

Notwithstanding some bumps in the road, Tesla uniquely fulfilled every requirement for extraordinary success identified by experts in the study of entrepreneurship. Yet it didn't leap to the top of the heap in 2019.

What was the additional piece that fell into place by the beginning of 2020?

The positive story really began to coalesce when Tesla surprised the market by reporting positive earnings in 2019's third quarter. Analysts had been expecting a third straight loss. The company's third-quarter 2019 flip to positive earnings occurred despite a drop in the average selling price of its flagship Model 3 sedan. Tesla attributed its turnaround to fundamental improvements in operating efficiency.

Tesla's operational upturn continued in the fourth quarter. So when the company announced another beat of analysts' adjusted earnings estimates on January 30, 2020, its stock soared by 53% in the space of just three trading sessions. Frantic short-covering contributed to the explosive move. At that point TSLA was the most heavily shorted U.S.-traded stock.

For the purpose of spotting future #1 stocks, it's useful to identify characteristics that elevated TSLA to its cream-of-the-crop status among all S&P 500 stocks over a 10-year period. To assist in your efforts, I've organized the company's story according to the themes indicated by the subheadings shown below.

Some of themes are ones you'll encounter with every stock you investigate. Others are unique to Tesla. Those ones aren't as transferable to the search for future top dogs, but they round out the story of how Tesla got to #1 in 2020.

Company Fundamentals

In the first week of January 2020 Tesla made a major step forward by starting delivery of its made-in-China Model 3 vehicles. Piper Sandler saw upside in TSLA, based on the potential to replicate in China the market-share success this model had achieved in the United States. Oppenheimer's Colin Rusch estimated that Tesla's products held a three-year competitive lead.

But Tesla's competitors weren't standing still. General Motors was planning a rollout of EVs that, at the top end, would exceed the range of any Tesla model. Things heated up some more when GM struck a deal to produce Nikola's marquee hydrogen fuel cell electric pickup truck in return for an 11% equity stake in Nikola.

When Tesla announced it fourth-quarter 2019 results, its beat on full-year 2019 deliveries guidance drew the most attention. Quarterly production set a record. TSLA's price surged in early February when Panasonic announced that its battery-producing joint venture with Tesla had achieved a quarterly profit for the first time.

In the second quarter Tesla once again beat on deliveries despite having to shut down its only U.S. factory because of the COVID-19 pandemic. In July, *Business Insider* proclaimed that the company had turned the corner on its past manufacturing problems. (As noted below, those difficulties had previously been a drag on TSLA's price.)

Tesla raised further hopes by scheduling a September Battery Day event. UBS analyst Patrick Hummel doubled his price target on the stock. He said Tesla's new cell technology was likely to cement its cost and technology advantage for several years. Hummel expected that the latest innovations would boost energy density by 50%, lowering cell costs per vehicle by $2,300 over the next three years.

On Battery Day CEO Musk claimed that Tesla's new technology would cut its battery cost in half and increase its vehicles' driving range by 16%. In the end, though, Battery Day was seen as a disappointment in light of the expectations that had been built up. TSLA sold off.

Analysts' Actions

Ali G, the dim-witted interviewer portrayed by comedian Sacha Baron Cohen, once asked former U.S. National Security Advisor Brent Scowcroft if he'd ever considered nuking Canada. Naturally, Scowcroft dismissed the idea as absurd. But the most amazing part of it, Ali G enthused, would be the element of surprise.

The outrageous humor created by Cohen's character depended on his interviewees not realizing that they were being hoaxed by a trickster intent on making them look ridiculous. Much as in Ali G's joke, the element of surprise can have an explosive effect on a stock's price, but it depends on there being a wide divergence of opinion.

If everybody already agrees that a company has outstanding management, surefire products, and a proven ability to execute on its brilliantly conceived business plan, there won't be much upside left in the stock price when management scores its next success.

Viewed through this lens, TSLA had lots of room to rise as 2020 began. The analysts weren't uniformly cheerleaders, as they so often are. At the beginning of the year, *Bloomberg News* actually reported more Sells (15) than Buys (11), with 10 Holds.

There wasn't any shortage of reasons to be cautious on TSLA. Three fatal crashes involving the company's Autopilot self-driving system had raised questions in regulators' minds about whether Tesla was doing enough to ensure that drivers were keeping their attention on the road. Tesla had captured 50% of the existing U.S. zero-emissions auto market with its EVs, but hydrogen cars posed a potential long-term competitive threat. Some experts saw risk in Tesla's use of very dense batteries that were composed of materials different from those used by other carmakers. And for years, Tesla had experienced snags in production, which was perceived to be of less interest to Elon Musk than technological breakthroughs.

David Einhorn of Greenlight Capital questioned the legitimacy of Tesla's accounting, asking why accounts receivable were so high at a company that got paid up front for its cars. Francine McKenna wrote in the accounting and audit newsletter *The Dig*, "No industry expert outside Tesla has expressed a belief that the company is anywhere close to deploying driverless cars." In the area of financial performance, JMP Securities expressed some concern about the gross margins that Tesla reported for 2019's fourth quarter. Yet another objection was that Tesla managed to post a profit in 2020's first quarter only by selling zero-emission air pollution credits to other automakers.

The stock's price sharp run-up during December and January fueled additional misgivings. Robert W. Baird analyst Ben Kallo pointed out that Tesla now had a market value greater than Ford and General Motors combined. He reduced his recommendation from Outperform to Neutral on valuation grounds and advised investors to take profits. CFRA went a step further, downgrading TSLA to Sell.

A *Bloomberg News* article by Ye Xie calculated that if Tesla were an S&P 500 member at that time, it would rank among the index's 10 most overpriced stocks, based on the technical metric known as the Relative Strength Indicator. A *Financial Times* headline read, "Tesla Is Nuts, Will It Ever Crash?" Former executive chairman of Templeton Emerging Markets Group Mark Mobius called Tesla's stock "scrip" and attributed its runup to "pure speculation." He said TSLA's valuation was now "off the roof."

Citigroup strategists included TSLA among the "bizarre valuation crossovers" induced by the rally in tech stocks. Cowen analyst Jeffrey Osborne said TSLA's valuation was "on Mars," although he bumped up his price target by 4% even as he kept his recommendation at Underperform. When Tesla beat on deliveries in the second quarter, RBC Capital Markets analyst Joe Spak calculated that the market applied an astronomical 47.5 times multiple to the increase in sales represented by the excess in deliveries over previous expectations.

Toward year-end JP Morgan's Ryan Brinkman presented some additional eye-popping statistics as signs of dramatic overvaluation. At the time, TSLA was priced at 1,325 times latest-12-months EPS, 291 times 2020 consensus estimates, and 175 times next-12-months' estimates. Of course, investors who were familiar with alternative metrics might have taken these outlandish numbers as definitive confirmation of Joel Stern's dictum that earnings per share don't count.

By late January, TSLA Sells outnumbered Buys, 17 to 9. The market didn't care. TSLA just kept going up.

Analysts who were more favorably disposed toward TSLA played catchup with the market action by increasing their price targets. Revisions implemented during January included boosts of 31% by Piper Sandler, 40% by Argus Research, 50% by Jefferies, 57% by Deutsche Bank, 59% by Oppenheimer, 70% by Credit Suisse, and 125% by Sanford

C. Bernstein. Morgan Stanley lifted its price target by 44% even as it downgraded TSLA to Underweight.

Canaccord Genuity hiked its target by 37% on January 2, putting that firm second only to New Street Research in its estimation of the upside in TSLA. Canaccord Genuity's comparatively optimistic revised price target, said *Business Insider*, meant the firm expected the stock to go up by a whopping 23% in 2020. The actual price change for the year turned out to be +743%.

This is to take nothing away from the conscientious work and solid analysis that surely went into Canaccord Genuity's price target revision. Appreciation of 23% in a year in which the S&P 500's price increase measured, say 16%, would have been an excellent result. The result would have earned Canaccord Genuity's research a well-deserved tip of the hat.

But someone attempting to pick 2020's top stock wouldn't have been put on TSLA's trail by a price target "only" 23% above the prevailing level. After all, the price changes of the previous three years' #1 stocks had ranged from +80% to +148%. (Note that these numbers were identical to the companies' total returns only if no dividends were paid.) The takeaway is that equity research can provide valuable insights into companies' operations and prospects, but scrutinizing analysts' price targets isn't a reliable method for spotting the next index-leading stock.

In Tesla's case, the above-mentioned market value comparison with Ford and General Motors was a turnoff for many analysts, as well as a lot of investors. After all, those industry kingpins sold many times more vehicles than Tesla. Weren't the biggest automakers inherently worth more than the minor players?

But such thinking missed the point, according to Elizabeth Knight, writing in the *Sydney Morning Herald*. She argued that the auto industry was in the midst of a radical transformation. In a similar vein, Morgan Stanley analyst Adam Jonas contended that TSLA's massive price appreciation coincided with forces that were hastening the end of the ICE Age, playing on the acronym for the internal combustion engine. Ross Gerber of TSLA shareholder Gerber Kawasaki Wealth and Investment Management argued that Tesla shouldn't be evaluated as a carmaker at all, but instead as a technology company.

In February 2020 Sundial Capital Research highlighted the happy fact that TSLA's 396% run over approximately the past eight months didn't yet match Qualcomm's "truly insane" 557% rally over a comparable period leading up to its early-January 2020 peak. CNBC's Jim Cramer said he wasn't even sure if TSLA was a stock. It appeared to him to be "something else entirely, like a new species discovered in the wild."

TSLA powered higher in the year's second half, prompting a five-for-one stock split and a plan by Tesla to sell another $5 billion of new shares. Inevitably, the price riot triggered another round of analysts' price target hikes. Dan Ives of Wedbush Securities, for example, jacked his target by 44% even as he remained at Neutral. Joseph Spak of RBC Capital upped his price target by 71% while staying at Underperform and calling Tesla's quality and service "below average." Going them one better, Adam Jonas of Morgan Stanley downgraded the stock from Equal Weight to Underweight at the same time as he boosted his price target by 30%. Phillipe Houchois of Jefferies, on the other hand, remained at Buy while more than doubling his price target. He said TSLA's "valuation exuberance" was justified and argued that the true valuation problem resided with its rivals, the legacy automakers.

Fortunately for investors who hadn't already bought TSLA, sharply divergent opinions preserved the potential for further short squeezing. JMP Securities president Mark Lehmann opined that the stock had obviously detached from its fundamentals. Argus Research's Bill Selesky expressed amazement that after he raised his 12-month price target, TSLA reached the new mark just one day later. In his opinion, the stock had risen too high, too fast. TSLA was "way out of control," he contended. "Mind-boggling" was the adjective chosen by Toni Sacconaghi of Sanford C. Bernstein as he downgraded TSLA from Market Perform to Underperform.

Bloomberg News, adhering to the view that EPS held the key to stock valuation, proclaimed a disconnect in the case of TSLA. In late July, the average analyst projection for adjusted EPS was down by about three-eighths from just four months earlier, yet the share price had quadrupled over the same period. For the very short run, the journalists' emphasis on the dubious metric EPS seemed to be vindicated. TSLA rose after the company announced a third-quarter EPS beat while missing on free cash flow. Interpreting the market's action was complicated, though, by the fact that the company simultaneously reported a beat on deliveries, a key investor focus in Tesla's case, as well as revenue. It's easy to leap from the one-day response to new EPS data to the conclusion that earnings per share drive valuation over the long run, contrary to Joel Stern's 1974 findings. Easy, that is, for those who've never heard of metrics such as the ones developed by Bennett Stewart, Valens Research, and others.

Price Volatility

TSLA forcefully demonstrated the principle that steady-as-a-rock stocks don't go to #1. Its price plunged by 61%

from its mid-February high to its lowest point for the year in March. As the share price faltered, analysts cut their price targets, with Wedbush Securities and Canacord Genuity slashing theirs by 43% and 47%, respectively. Despite those swings, the stock still managed to finish up 25% for the first quarter.

By the end of the second quarter, TSLA's price was up by 199% from its mid-March low. TSLA rose another 99% in the third quarter and by a further 65% in the fourth. Those advances occurred despite a 34% plunge in September's first five trading days.

One way to quantify volatility is to calculate the standard deviation of daily prices as a percentage of the average price for the period. For the S&P 500, this measure was 10% during 2020. TSLA checked in at 58%, making it massively more volatile than the market as a whole.

Credit Quality Improvement

Tesla's credit quality was recognizably on the upswing before 2020 dawned, a favorable indication for its future stock performance. The company's liquidity improved in during 2019, as Bloomberg Intelligence's Joel Levington noted. Debt investors shared that upbeat view. Yields on Tesla's bonds declined toward year-end 2019, confirming that the market perceived reduced credit risk.

Early in 2020 the company reported that it had $6.3 billion of cash as of the end of 2019's fourth quarter, up from just under $1 billion three months earlier. Cash flow was positive in the last three quarters of 2019. Tesla's financial strength gained further when the company announced plans to raise $2 billion in equity. The company announced two more equity sales over the course of the year, impervious to criticisms that it seemed to be requiring a lot of new funds for a company at such an advanced stage. (For fixed income investors, though, the more the company fattened it equity balance, the better.)

S&P Global Ratings analyst Nishit Madlani indicated in early February that an upgrade was possible before year end. Moody's acted sooner than that, upgrading Tesla from B3 to B2 in July. S&P followed suit in October with an upgrade from B+ to BB-, citing improved liquidity and competitiveness. In December, S&P upgraded Tesla one more notch, to BB with a Positive outlook.

Joining the S&P 500

Although TSLA more than qualified for inclusion in the S&P 500 by one key criterion, it didn't join the index until the tail end of 2020. Before it finally got the nod, TSLA's total market value would have placed it in the index's top 10 stocks by that measure. The main stumbling block was that Tesla had never satisfied the qualification of stringing together four consecutive quarters of GAAP profitability.

As 2020 progressed, it appeared likely that Tesla would finally achieve that feat. The prospect of being added to the S&P 500 became part of the bulls' case for the stock. *Investor's Business Daily* reported that among the 14 stocks added to the index through late October, the average gain was roughly double the S&P 500's comparable-period gain. This performance edge, which TSLA stood to enjoy upon its anointment, was commonly attributed at least in part to index funds needing to buy S&P 500 newbies' shares in order to continue matching their reference indexes.

Finally, in 2020's second quarter, Tesla posted its fourth consecutive quarterly profit. The composition of the S&P 500 isn't, however, based entirely on quantitative rules. At its next regularly scheduled meeting, S&P Dow Jones Indices disappointingly chose not to add TSLA. The stock reacted with its biggest-ever one-day loss.

Then, in November, when TSLA was finally cleared to join the S&P 500 beginning in December, it jumped by 13% in after-hours trading. TSLA became the S&P 500's largest-ever new constituent on December 21, just in time to qualify as the index's #1 stock for 2020. TSLA also replaced Occidental Petroleum in the S&P 100, a subset of the larger index that tracks the performance of major U.S. blue chip companies.

Milestones

During 2020 Tesla officially became the most valuable U.S. carmaker of all time. As its shares continued to levitate, Tesla overtook Volkswagen AG in market value for the first time, leaving it behind only Toyota on the global stage. Tesla then passed Boeing to become the largest U.S. industrial company by market value.

Meanwhile, Elon Musk overtook Bill Gates to become the world's second-richest person behind Jeff Bezos. Musk began the year at #35 on the list, a testament to the enormousness of TSLA's rise. All in all, it had proven fortunate for Musk that when he attempted to sell the company to Apple during the darkest days of its Model 3 program, Apple CEO Tim Cook declined the meeting. Since that time, TSLA had risen to 10 times its earlier price. Closing the loop, *Investor's Business Daily* reported in late 2020 that TSLA had overtaken AAPL as the most popular stock held by millennials.

Elon Musk's Unique Leadership Style

Elon Musk didn't guest-host *Saturday Night Live* until 2021 but he still differentiated himself from the typical corporate CEO in numerous ways in 2020. When the company celebrated the commencement of shipments from its

Shanghai factory, Musk tweeted a 15-second clip of himself performing a striptease-style dance at the event. *Business Insider* labeled his moves "robotic." On May Day, Musk triggered a 10% decline in TSLA by saying its price had gotten too high.

Another corporate leader might have been embarrassed by the 2019 product demo gone wrong in which the supposedly invincible Cybertruck got dented. Musk instead laughed it off. Tesla began marketing a $45 "bulletproof" tee-shirt with an image of broken glass on the front and the Cybertruck logo on the back.

Musk once again exhibited his distinctive sense of humor when he announced a price cut on Tesla's flagship Model S. The new price, $69,420, combined references to a sexual position and marijuana consumption. (A group of Californian teenagers had ritualistically smoked weed every day at 4:20 p.m. and 4/20 eventually became a marijuana holiday.) Asked in an interview by Axel Springer CEO Mathias Döpfner why he'd expressed a desire to be buried on Mars, Musk replied, "If you're going to be buried somewhere, it would be cool to be born on Earth and die on Mars—just not on impact."[1]

Never reticent about his views on just about any subject, Musk called for a breakup of Amazon. An outspoken critic of the public policy response to the COVID-19 epidemic (he labeled the government-mandated quarantine "fascist"), Musk was incensed by the case of an author who claimed that Amazon had yanked his book on that subject. Musk went on to call Amazon founder Bezos a copycat when Amazon acquired the self-driving car startup Zoox.

On the side, Musk engaged in a Twitter feud with a former U.S. Secretary of Labor. Robert Reich labeled him a "modern day robber baron." Musk, who'd stoutly resisted unionization, responded by calling Reich a "modern day moron." Bill Gates became another verbal sparring partner after opining that electric power would "probably never be a practical solution for things like 28-wheelers, cargo ships, and passenger jets." Musk replied that Gates had no clue.

Like him or hate him, Elon Musk contributed to Tesla brand loyalty through his big personality. Late in 2020 the company entered a new business line by offering a limited edition of the Tesla Tequila. The supply sold out in a matter of hours, and some of the empty lightning-bolt-shaped bottles offered on eBay attracted bids in excess of $700. (One sold for $1,420.69, recycling Musk's in-joke involving the Model S price cut.) Having a CEO in the Elon Musk mold is by no means a prerequisite for achieving the distinction of ranking as the #1 S&P 500 stock. But the members of that exclusive club do tend to stand out from their lesser-performing peers, one way or another.

2021: Devon Energy (DVN) +196%

At first glance, there's no great mystery about why the oil and gas exploration and production (E&P) company Devon Energy catapulted from #481 in the S&P 500, ranked by price change, in 2020 to #1 in 2021. The crude oil price (West Texas Intermediate) dropped by 20.5% in 2020 as Saudi Arabia stepped up production. The OPEC leader hoped to reduce competition by running U.S. shale oil producers into the ground. Then, in 2021, crude shot up by 81%. On the back of those violent swings, Energy was the S&P 500's biggest loser one year and its biggest gainer the next. Seemingly, all you had to do to tag DVN as a massive winner in 2021 was correctly predict the huge oil price climb. Easier said than done.

But a lot of energy companies that also benefited from the commodity price rise didn't top 499 other stocks in the S&P 500 in 2021. Devon Energy must have had some distinctive features. Indeed it did, and those features sound a lot like the special ingredients that our other #1 stocks had.

To be completely clear, you shouldn't count on an E&P company producing a super return without a huge surge in energy prices. But that's something that happens every so often in the extremely volatile market for oil and gas. In 20% of the years from 2007 to 2021, Energy was the top performer among the S&P 500's 11 sectors. So, aside from picking your candidate for #1, it doesn't hurt to have at least one stock in your portfolio that's particularly well positioned to benefit from a spike in oil and gas prices.

Several things made Devon stand out from the E&P pack during 2020's bleak days. First was the edge associated with being a low-cost producer. Second was a comparatively strong balance sheet that differentiated Devon in an industry that relies heavily on borrowed money. Devon amplified both advantages in advance of 2021's oil price rebound. But what truly set the company apart from its industry peers in its championship year was a change in management's operating and financial strategy, which was instituted in conjunction with a late-2020 merger.

At the outset of 2020 Devon's fans were pointing out that the company had sold lower-yielding, longer-payback properties to reinvest in more promising shale oil activities and to fund stock buybacks. This strategic shift was part of a growing demand from energy investors for near-term improvements in return on equity. Devon was not unique in responding to those demands, but it was perceived to be ahead of many competitors in adopting new, more efficient drilling technologies.

As for Devon's relatively clean balance sheet, analysts saw it as giving the company the inside track on acquiring attractive drilling prospects during difficult times. Devon entered 2020 with $1.8 billion in cash and a $3 billion undrawn credit facility. With no debt coming due before 2025, Devon had outstanding financial flexibility, enabling it to continue bearing down on improving its operating efficiency.[2]

On January 2, 2020, Bloomberg Intelligence's Talon Custer and Vincent G. Piazza cited these factors in a report hailing the "New Devon." They highlighted the free cash flow (the key to stock valuation, remember, according to Joel Stern) generated by the company's Eagle Ford shale play. Custer and Piazza further noted that management's commitment to returning profits to shareholders included substantial stock buybacks.

Devon's good story got even better as 2020 wore on. Management engineered a merger with WPX Energy, with Devon as the continuing company. The deal added reasonably adjacent properties, facilitating additional operating efficiencies on top of those already achieved. The combined company also gained economies of scale by eliminating redundancies in corporate overhead.

Rather than borrow to acquire WPX, Devon negotiated a stock-for-stock transaction in which it paid a very modest premium to WPX's prevailing share price. The deal added WPX's debt to the balance sheet, yet Moody's raised the outlook on Devon's credit rating from Stable to Positive. The credit agency cited the company's plans for reducing that added debt load.

As it engineered the WPX transaction, Devon inaugurated a new dividend policy that was the first of its kind within the energy industry. Along with a fixed quarterly dividend, DVN would pay to shareholders 50% of the free cash flow that remained after the fixed payment. That innovation further differentiated Devon from its peers by providing its shareholders an exceptionally high dividend yield.

It's important to recognize how revolutionary—although simple—a departure this was from the way E&P companies had traditionally operated. The standard practice was to respond to a surge in oil and gas prices by plowing a sudden influx of extra cash into increased production. Why not take full advantage of the higher prices, managers reasoned, by having more oil and gas to sell? Unfortunately, by stepping up production, the companies increased supply while demand held steady, forcing prices to fall. The dollars invested in boosting production consequently earned mediocre returns.

An alternative to investing the windfall from a sudden jump in energy prices would have been to deliver the benefit directly to shareholders by increasing the dividend. The problem with that approach was that because E&P profits are so volatile, a big hike in the dividend rate would prove unsustainable. A year or two later, the company would have to cut its payout, making its stock a pariah to investors.

Devon broke out of this bind by splitting its dividend into fixed and variable components. The extra-large dividend paid in a boom year would return to a more normal level, along with receding energy prices. But so long as management explained the plan clearly, investors wouldn't be turned off to the stock when that happened.

As the company grew, it could raise the fixed portion of the dividend at a sustainable rate. Barring a more permanent setback to the business, this new measure would provide investors the comfort of a floor on the payout. For investors who liked having temporarily elevated profits returned to them instead of invested in a way that was doomed to earn a low return on capital, Devon Energy was the only game in town.

All in all, DVN stood out from the E&P crowd. It was exceptionally well positioned to benefit from a rebound in oil prices. As I have already noted, that rebound came with a vengeance in 2021. It became clear that Saudi Arabia had failed in its attempt to snuff out the U.S. shale industry by flooding the market with supply.

Energy stocks rallied mightily, but DVN more mightily than any other. It was no fluke. Analysts had identified well in advance the characteristics that made DVN a top pick within its group. They were low-cost production, balance sheet strength, and innovation in the area of dividend policy.

Analysts who were bullish on DVN provided a genuine benefit to investors by showing how the company was especially well positioned if energy prices were to surge in 2021. In some cases, their beginning-of-year price targets also represented good advice. Among analysts polled by Capital IQ, some called for a price move as great as 137%. That was still shy of the actual +196% move achieved by DVN during 2021, but the bulls had the right idea.

Other analysts began the year with price targets below DVN's 2020 year-end level. That provided the diversity of opinion that makes it possible for fulfillment of the optimistic predictions to move the stock. But regardless of where they started out, analysts had the opportunity to hike their price targets as events unfolded more favorably than they reckoned on.

Many did switch course and boost their PTs. There's nothing to find fault with about that. Analysts served investors better by changing their minds when the facts changed than they would have by stubbornly clinging to their original outlooks.

Still, there wouldn't have been any need for upward revisions of price targets if the analysts and their commodity-forecasting colleagues could have foreseen the magnitude of the 2021 rise in the benchmark West Texas Intermediate (WTI) crude oil price. As a group, they didn't. With WTI at

$48.52 on December 31, 2020, the median forecast reported by the New York Mercantile Exchange was $42.00.

The forecasters may have been influenced by WTI's 21% drop from $61.06 one year earlier. But instead of registering a small further decline in 2021, WTI soared by 55% to finish at $75.21. Based on the consensus outlook, nobody would have expected DVN to lead the S&P 500 in 2021.

This isn't to suggest that the oil price prognosticators failed to apply the accepted methods correctly. The 2021 surprise simply underscored the impossibility of *consistently* forecasting oil prices with accuracy. Making one or two "great calls" in a row doesn't qualify. That degree of success may be purely the result of luck. Being right about one huge swing may, however, earn a media appellation, as in, "The genius who predicted the last big move in oil prices now says . . ."

It's rational for the manager of a business that's sensitive to fuel costs to get experts' best estimates of future oil prices, based on the information available at the time. But you shouldn't count on the forecasters to tip you off when energy prices are poised to begin another meteoric rise. In any given year, the best-positioned energy company within the S&P 500 may wind up being the index's biggest winner, as Devon Energy did in 2021. Energy prices are a wild card when it comes to finding the #1 stock.

On February 16, as if to support Joel Stern's insistence on the irrelevance of EPS to stock valuation, Devon reported an earnings miss for 2020's fourth quarter. Analysts, traders, and the media might have been waiting for the numbers with bated breath, but in the scheme of things they hardly mattered. Prior to the earnings release the stock was up 26% on the year, and it rallied further despite the miss. JPMorgan explained the post-announcement rise as a response to Devon commencing its special dividend sooner than expected. The company said it would pay $0.19 a share in addition to the regular $0.11 payout.

Later in the year Devon stated that it expected to have the highest dividend yield in the entire S&P 500 Index and might consider boosting its regular dividend in 2022. In addition, the company's board of directors authorized $1 billion of share repurchases through the end of 2022. CEO Rick Muncrief said that Devon's top-in-class dividend remained the top priority, but buybacks provided another way to return value to shareholders and enhance results on a per-share basis.

Shareholders got some more good news on March 11 as Devon announced that it would pay off $700 million of debt obligations earlier than their stated maturity dates. Moody's shortly afterwards upgraded its outlook for the company's bond rating from Stable to Positive. That action solidified

Devon's status as an improving credit, a trait it shared with some previous #1 stocks.

Later in 2021 Standard & Poor's, too, raised its outlook to Positive. Moody's upgraded Devon's rating from Ba1 to Baa3. The rating change lifted Devon to the investment-grade category. That kind of shift broadens the market for a company's bonds, since many funds are limited in their ability to buy speculative-grade securities.

Debt holders were less enthusiastic about Devon's early redemption of a large chunk of its debt, spread across three issues. This wasn't received as enthusiastically by the debt holders. The redemption prices were well below the notes' recent trading prices. According to the securities' indentures, holders were protected against early redemption except in the event that Devon raised equity for that purpose. Devon contended that its all-stock merger with WPX qualified as raising equity.

The Credit Roundtable, an industry group for bond investors, vehemently disagreed. It urged its members to demand stricter indenture language in future underwritings. Otherwise, companies would be able to exploit the loophole in order to benefit shareholders at the expense of bond holders. No one could dispute, however, that Devon's management was exerting itself to benefit shareholders. Equity analysts heartily approved, with some raising their price targets by 21% to 38% during March.

Toward the end of that month, Devon's sector caught a lucky break. A container ship got stuck in the Suez Canal, blocking a key route for international oil transport. Crude prices, which had been sliding, suddenly turned back up, boosting energy stocks. Calamity-driven events of this sort are unforeseeable in predicting which stock will reach #1. But they're warmly welcomed by shareholders of the companies that Fortune has smiled upon, if not always by the rest of the population.

Over the next few months, analysts' price targets continued to parallel the upward climb of DVN's actual price. Upward revisions were typically on the order of 10% to 20% but ranged as high as nearly 50% at a crack. By early November, Buys outnumbered Sells 26 to 1, with 5 Holds.

Contributing to the EPS-minded analysts' optimism was a string of beats in the last three quarters. An upbeat industry outlook further stoked their enthusiasm. In upgrading DVN from Inline to Outperform, Evercore ISI's Stephen Richardson proclaimed a "new paradigm" for the E&P sector. He called Energy the "top of the whip" in the "reopening trade," a reference to the economy's expected pickup as it emerged from the COVID-19 pandemic. Jim Cramer tapped DVN as a better vehicle than the major oil companies for playing a crude price rise to $100 a barrel.

As is frequently the case with oil prices, political developments entered the picture during DVN's triumphal year.

Immediately after taking the reins in Washington, D.C., the Biden administration sought to fulfill a campaign promise by imposing a 60-day moratorium on the issuance of new oil and gas drilling permits on federal lands. Fortunately, the impact on prospective E&P revenues was limited. Anticipating such an action, the companies had loaded up on leases ahead of the 2020 election. In June the U.S. Court of Appeals issued a preliminary injunction to lift the moratorium. Then, in August, a hearing on the merits produced a ruling that obliged the administration to resume leasing oil and gas rights on federal lands.

In summary, DVN's index-leading total return for the year represented a remarkable turnaround. In the months prior to the company's merger with WPX in September 2020, its stock had been one of the S&P 500's worst performers. The rebound in energy prices catapulted the energy sector to the top of the heap in 2021 and Devon excelled within that group through a profound change in its corporate philosophy. Management sent an unequivocal message to investors that it would return free cash flow to them through a clearly laid out fixed-plus-variable dividend framework.

Chapter Three

News Flash! There Are More Than 500 Stocks

S&P 500 STOCKS ARE THIS book's primary focus, but there's a wider world beyond that index. The stocks discussed in this chapter joined the S&P 500 between 2020 and 2021, but before that happened, they outperformed all S&P 500 stocks in the indicated years. Their stories provide additional clues for investors who want to try their hand at identifying #1 stocks in advance.

This topic is also important because of the unusual outcome of 2020's race to the top. The stock that eventually captured the #1 spot, TSLA, wasn't in the S&P 500 when the year began. On any given December 31, the coming year's champion may be waiting in the wings, hoping for its chance to knock some other stock out of the charmed circle of half-a-thousand large-cap U.S.-listed stocks.

Suppose you identify a promising stock that's not yet in the S&P 500 and want to figure out if it has a shot at getting in. Standard & Poor's publishes detailed guidelines for inclusion, but the key characteristics you should look for are the following:

1. The company must satisfy a minimum market capitalization test. As of 2022 it's set at $14.6 billion. This number has risen and—in 2008—fallen over time. Standard & Poor's reports 13 changes since 2007. In each case, the new minimum threshold was equivalent to 0.3% of the S&P 500's level on the date of the change. This should work as a rule of thumb for determining if your candidate company has a shot at inclusion in the event of another change in the threshold.

2. At least 10% of all the company's shares must be included among the shares that trade publicly.

(Management and pre-IPO investors may own a large number of unregistered shares.)

3. The company's most recent quarterly earnings and the sum of its four trailing consecutive quarterly earning must both be positive.

Bear in mind that the Standard & Poor's index committee doesn't simply apply these rules in a mechanical fashion. In 2020, Tesla reported a fourth consecutive positive quarter. Many investors expected its stock to join the S&P 500 at the index committee's next meeting, but it didn't happen until later that year.

Here are the stories of some companies that beat all S&P 500 companies within a few years before entering their ranks. They contribute usefully to the next chapter's distillation of the traits that have characterized top stocks.

2017: SolarEdge Technologies (SEDG) 203%

SolarEdge Technologies competes in the field of solar power equipment. The Israeli company is known especially for inverters and optimizers. Inverters transform the direct current (DC) electricity produced by solar panels to the alternating current (AC) electricity used by the power grid.

Optimizers maximize the amount of energy harvested from solar photovoltaic systems.

At the end of 2016 SolarEdge's stock price was 31% below its March 25, 2015, IPO price. Over that same interval, by contrast, the S&P 500 rose by 9%. Following a 56% plunge in calendar 2016, was there *any* hint that this (at the time) S&P 500 outsider was poised to triple in 2017, beating every single stock in the index?

Without a doubt, SolarEdge had taken some hard knocks since it went public. Both coal and natural gas prices fell by 19% in 2015, according to Bloomberg, dampening demand for solar power. Competition from Chinese solar producers was intensifying. Furthermore, SolarEdge was locked in a price war with its archrival Enphase Energy as solar roof installations slowed.

In November 2016, the biggest buyer of SolarEdge's photovoltaic systems, Elon Musk's SolarCity, announced that it would scale back its installation of panels. On top of that, SolarCity indicated that once it completed its planned merger with Tesla, it would start building the components that it had been buying from SolarEdge. Compounding these worries, investors were unhappy about the concentration of SolarEdge's business, customer-wise, with SolarCity and geographically within the United States.

But true to its name, the company had an edge in the solar business—superior technology. In November 2015

Avondale Partners analyst Michael Morosi identified SolarEdge as the low-cost producer. The company possessed the kind of technology, he said, that enabled it to chip away at costs, offsetting the potential loss of renewable energy subsidies. And in 2016 SolarEdge rolled out a new residential integrated optimizer/inverter model. It had half the weight of its predecessor, as well as greater efficiency, and generated less heat. Experts saw potential for a surge in demand for SolarEdge products, particularly in Germany and Australia.

While SolarEdge's share price faced strong headwinds prior to its 2017 breakout, its financial performance was generally good. The company consistently beat analysts' earnings estimates throughout 2015 and 2016. Solar energy companies got some relief in 2016 as the prices of coal and natural gas roared back, rising by 75% and 59%, respectively. And in a technical development that was likely to facilitate an upswing, the number of shorted SEDG shares as a percentage of the total outstanding hit a record high late in 2016.

There was no guarantee that SolarEdge's fortunes would change in 2017. Otherwise, its stock wouldn't have been languishing so far below its IPO level. But the company possessed certain characteristics that distinguished it from the hordes of others that would almost certainly never reach #1 on the hit parade over a full-year period.

Helpfully, a lot of things went right for SolarEdge In 2017. The shares surged in February on a revenue beat, even though adjusted EPS fell short of analysts' consensus forecast by a penny. JMP Securities analyst Joseph Osha noted, as he upgraded the stock from Market Perform to Outperform in March, that competitor Enphase was becoming smaller. Also, previous rumors that Chinese rival Huawei Technologies would enter the rooftop market hadn't been vindicated.

Soon SolarEdge was beating even the highest EPS estimates. Solid earnings enabled the company to beef up its cash balance. With no debt on its balance sheet, the company's financial flexibility represented an advantage over its beleaguered competitors. SolarEdge had greater freedom to invest in product development and geographical expansion, as well as to consider strategic acquisitions.

Analysts began upgrading their recommendations and boosting their price targets. Roth Capital's Philip Shen raised his by 62.5% in July. In November Carter Driscoll of B. Riley increased his target by 150% while upgrading his recommendation from Neutral to Buy and praising management's "near flawless execution." When Canaccord Genuity analyst Colin Rusch stepped up his price target in August he noted that SolarEdge was delivering what investors wanted, conspicuously large upside.

One factor that analysts cited in their PT hikes was SolarEdge's technological leadership. The company reinforced that reputation by introducing the world's first inverter-integrated electric vehicle charger. Its Level 2 device supplemented grid power with photovoltaic power to make EV charging up to six times faster than the standard process. Analysts also saw big growth opportunities for SolarEdge, which had initially focused on the residential market, in the commercial and industrial sectors.

SolarEdge caught some breaks in 2017. A big one was a delay in Huawei's rollout of a competing optimizer. In late July, European customers hadn't received the product, and it was unclear when U.S. shipments would begin.

U.S. solar manufacturers did manage to convince the International Trade Commission that they were being harmed by foreign competition. The ITC recommended a 30% to 35% tariff on crystalline solar panels to President Trump. But this was seen as less damaging than a worst-case outcome.

As the same time, SolarEdge was making its own breaks. To contend with Enphase's step-up in price competition, it worked to cut costs. Management adopted an asset-lite structure, outsourcing production of its power optimizer. That reduced SolarEdge's capital burden, further enhancing its financial flexibility.

By late November, many former SEDG skeptics had thrown in the towel. The stock was up by more than 200% from its previous year-end level. Deutsche Bank analyst Vishal Shah concluded that the market was fully pricing in the prospect of excellent execution in both the solar and non-solar segments. He therefore downgraded SEDG from Buy to Hold.

The stock responded with a 12% decline, its biggest in more than 14 months. But it made back a portion of that loss in December. SEDG's full-year gain of 203% (identical to its total return, as it paid no dividend) outdid all 500 stocks in S&P's flagship index.

2018: Etsy (ETSY) 133%

Like SolarEdge Technologies, Etsy went public in 2015 and promptly saw its stock price nosedive. By the end of 2015, IPO buyers were underwater to the tune of 48%. The online marketer of handmade and vintage goods had a dark cloud hanging over it.

Like many other retailers, Etsy was up against the Amazon Effect. With 400 times the sales of Etsy in 2017, the merchandising world's 800-pound gorilla had the wherewithal to barge into, and possibly take over, the lesser-resourced firm's category. In the same year that Etsy went public, Amazon went into competition with the smaller company by launching its Amazon Handmade program.

The specter of the retailing behemoth potentially siphoning off a major portion of Etsy's revenues dampened analysts' enthusiasm for its shares. Critics maintained that Etsy appealed only to niche customers making occasional purchases. It didn't help that during 2015–2016 Etsy had reported only a single quarter of positive earnings.

Events of 2017, however, set the stage for ETSY's chart-topping gain the following year. Several activist investors, beginning with Black-and-White Capital, began taking large stakes and pressing management for changes aimed at boosting the stock price. When TPG Capital and Dragoneer amassed a combined 8% position and offered to engage in talks on strategic alternatives, ETSY shares rallied to their biggest one-day gain in nine months.

Soon afterward, management disclosed that it was working with Goldman Sachs on a strategic review. In August, *Deal Reporter* said that several private equity firms had approached Etsy and that the company appeared open to being acquired. Earlier in the year, Shelly Banjo of *Bloomberg Editorial* had suggested that Etsy would be a good fit for eBay. Takeover speculation helped lift ETSY back to its IPO price by August 2017.

Besides fanning takeover speculation, the activists helped to bring about sweeping internal change at Etsy. In May 2017 the company replaced its CEO with eBay veteran Josh Silverman, who immediately announced plans to reduce the workforce by 8%. That target later rose to a total of 22% for the year. Going forward, Etsy would cut spending on vendors, consultants, and assorted internal programs to focus on growth.

The company was responding to investors' pressures to stop spending like a tech startup and start acting like a retailer. Management began relying to a greater extent than formerly on technology developed elsewhere, moving away from what the *Wall Street Journal* had called "guerilla-type marketing" and a "do-it-all-yourself engineering culture." Along with the new operating style came a new chief financial officer and chief technology officer.

The Amazon Effect hadn't entirely disappeared, but by early 2017 Loop Capital analyst Blake Harper asserted that Etsy had accomplished the rare feat of fending off competition from the online retailing Goliath through investments in artificial intelligence. Those initiatives enabled Etsy to aid buyer search and upgrade its product listings with more descriptive labels. Etsy also had goodwill with sellers, who were charged a fee of only 3.5% of their selling prices plus $0.20 per product listing versus a 15% fee at Amazon. Later in the year, Amazon attempted to turn up the competitive heat by launching its Handmade Gift Shop, targeting holiday and special-occasion shoppers. The Handmade Gift Shop enabled shoppers to search by categories such as "for her" and "for baby" and by price range.

Meanwhile, Etsy improved its financial performance, posting only its second profitable quarter as a public company in 2017's second quarter. In the third quarter the company's revenue beat the highest analyst estimate, and

EPS walloped the consensus, $0.21 to $0.06. ETSY jumped by 21.5% in December 2017. The momentum had clearly shifted. Even if the further developments that propelled the shares in 2018 weren't all foreseeable, ETSY was starting to look like one of the small minority of stocks with supreme stock leadership potential.

As Etsy began to realize that potential, analysts boosted their price targets. Scott Devitt of Stifel Nicolaus raised his target by one-third, even while leaving his recommendation at Hold. He noted the company's "enhanced marketing capabilities" and "search/discoverability improvements." In March 2018, the lone analyst with an Underweight rating on ETSY, Morgan Stanley's Brian Nowak, acknowledged that Etsy had carved itself a niche outside Amazon's core competency and was therefore relatively immune to disruption by its much bigger rival.

Also in March, Loop Capital analyst Laura Champine characterized CEO Josh Silverman's experience at eBay as a boon to Etsy's efforts toward further improvement in the buyer experience. Additional gains could be achieved, she contended, by improving the company's search engine. So far, Champine said, Etsy searches were a hit-or-miss proposition. More filtering was needed to help shoppers deal with the platform's 50 million items. For investors, this additional upside represented a reason to assign ETSY a high earnings multiple.

By June 1, ETSY was up 55% on the year. That month the company raised its seller fee from 3.5% to 5%. The share price soared by 33% in June.

CEO Silverman later reported that sellers hadn't rebelled over the fee hike. There was almost no perceptible change in their behavior in terms of churn rates or item pricing. (In conjunction with the increase, Etsy had introduced new tools and packages for sellers.) Meanwhile, company initiatives to improve customer experience had led to higher repeat-buying rates and improved advertising had generated more first-time customers.

Additional analysts initiated coverage, and Etsy continued to rack up earnings beats. The company had a microscopic miss in the third quarter, but it also reported its fourth consecutive quarter of accelerating gross merchandise sales. ETSY made a new all-time high. What's more, its outstanding performance proved not to be a one-time affair. ETSY entered the S&P 500 during 2020 and ranked fourth in return that year among all stocks in the index.

2019: Enphase Energy (ENPH) 452%

We last encountered Enphase Energy embroiled in a fierce competitive battle with the other leading producer of solar microinverters for the residential market, SolarEdge, a spectacular performer in 2017. ENPH went through a tough period in the mid-2010s, ending 2016 at a level 83% below its 2012 initial public offering price. From that point, the stock more than doubled in 2017 and nearly doubled again in 2018. Among the S&P 500's #1 stocks covered in the previous chapter, ENPH's 2019 gain of +452% was surpassed only by Tesla's +743% gain the following year.

What accounts for such stellar performance over so extended a period? And why, after back-to-back gains in the range of 100% was there still enough juice in the battery to propel ENPH to its best year of all? As with other top stocks, innovation and a competitive edge were key elements of the story.

As 2018 began, commentators were hailing the profit potential of technological advances in solar power. Demand for solar inverter suppliers such as Enphase was expanding thanks to a mouthful called *module-level power electronics* (MLPE). This technology was revolutionizing the control and monitoring of system performance. In January 2018 Enphase began delivering the seventh generation of its IQ line. It was 19% lighter and 17% smaller than the previous model, while delivering 4% more power.

But translating technological improvements into higher profits was no simple task. Competition was speeding up cuts in product costs. To make matters worse, existing producers faced possible disruption by new U.S. and Chinese entrants to the market. Much as Etsy shares had been held down for a time by the threat of incursion from Amazon, the 800-pound gorilla of online retailing, SolarEdge and Enphase were threatened by the electronics industry's 800-pound panda, Huawei Technologies. Already dominant in inverters for utility-scale projects, the Chinese giant began shipping products for the residential market, where SolarEdge and Enphase focused, after a year-long delay.

Also hanging over Enphase's inverter business in early 2018 was a newly imposed U.S. tariff on solar panels. Enphase didn't produce solar panels, but it shipped microinverters to Asia to be attached onto panels produced there and sold in the United States. Based on this arrangement, the company sought an exemption from the new tariff.

Later in 2018, the tariff was increased. Vertical Group analyst Gordon Johnson called this development an "incremental negative" for companies such as Enphase and SolarEdge that owned or outsourced manufacturing capacity in China. European-based manufacturers, which had recently upgraded their technology, were likely to benefit at those companies' expense, said Johnson. On the other hand, Enphase benefited from its arrangement as exclusive supplier of microinverters to SunPower, which managed to obtain a tariff exemption.

In December 2018, Enphase caught a break when Huawei's incursion into the U.S. rooftop solar market hit a snag. Huawei's chief financial officer was arrested in Canada for potential violation of U.S. trade sanctions on Iran. That event, coming at a critical juncture in U.S.-Chinese trade negotiations, represented a potential setback for Huawei's expansion into the residential market. B. Riley Financial analyst Carter Driscoll pointed out an additional obstacle to Huawei's ambitions: Because smart inverters are designed to be controlled remotely, concerns were being raised that a Chinese company would potentially be able to manipulate power on America's electricity grids.

Along with these setbacks to Huawei's initiatives, Enphase appeared to be gaining ground technologically against its main established competitor, SolarEdge. Williams Research Partners analyst Brad Meikle's channel checks indicated that Enphase was one to two quarters ahead of SolarEdge in the manufacturing transition then underway. T.J. Roberts, writing on the *Seeking Alpha* website in September 2018, described Enphase as the clear leader in the solar MLPE technology mentioned several paragraphs back. He reported that veteran solar installers were enthusiastic about the eighth generation of Enphase's IQ line, which was out by then. Unlike all other competing products, Enphase's could operate without batteries, making it the low-cost option. Customer adoption of the new technology had taken some time, but it was now picking up.

With its existing customers alone representing a market for upgrading of hundreds of millions of dollars, Enphase would go into 2019 with huge, as-yet-unrealized, growth opportunities. The conditions for a spectacular year were further enhanced by a substantial and rising short interest in ENPH. That partly reflected the stock's 96% rise in 2018 to a level many investors evidently thought amounted to too much too soon.

The skeptics proved wrong. In 2019 Enphase caught a wave of investor excitement about solar power. Through the year's first 10 months, Invesco Solar ETF (TAN) was the year's biggest gainer among all exchange-traded funds. It didn't hurt that the S&P 500 as a whole rose by 29%, the largest percentage price gain within our five-year period of most intensive focus. But ENPH reigned supreme in the S&P index and among solar-related stocks on the strength of company-specific achievements.

Less than one full month into the year, Enphase announced that it had strengthened its financial position by paying off all its term loan debt. The company generally exceeded analysts' expectations, particularly on adjusted gross margin, a key metric in light of concerns about competitive pressures. As ENPH rose, it attracted new coverage and benefited from target price increases.

The stock proverbially climbed a wall of worry. After Enphase shifted some production to Mexico in response to continually rising tariffs on Chinese solar panels, the Trump administration imposed a tariff on Mexican imports.

Enphase was constrained in passing along that cost increase because of some competitors' tariff-free production in Southeast Asia. Short-sellers targeted Enphase, making disputed claims of inventory backup in the company's distribution channels and pointing to energy titan Generac's entry into the residential solar market. Stock sales by Enphase's chief financial officer and chief executive officer took some of the shine off a favorable insider buying trend.

None of these developments prevented Enphase from beating all S&P 500 stocks in 2019. The stock achieved that distinction despite a 25% pullback from its August 21 high. Enphase simply had a lot of the traits that propelled certain stocks to the top of the heap throughout the period covered by our analysis.

Chapter Four

Tip-Offs to Top Stocks

~

THE PREVIOUS TWO CHAPTERS explained how S&P 500 #1 stocks and a few other spectacular performers achieved one-year total returns ranging from 80% to 743%. Even more important, they described each company's characteristics in the year prior to its superlative performance. Those are the traits you need to look for to identify next year's top stock.

This chapter distills from their stories the key markers of future #1s. An essential part of your search for the crème de la crème consists of eliminating the vast majority of

S&P 500 stocks that don't fit the profile. I'll detail some statistical measures that will help you identify the genuine contenders. These selection rules are drawn from a longer list of possible quantitative criteria that I tested with the help of John Lee, the data manager on this project. Once you've applied them so that you can zero in on your prime candidates, you can move on to the qualitative factors discussed later in the chapter.

Before I run through the statistical and qualitative selection factors, though, let me once again stress a key point made in Chapter One, "Forget About Conventional Analysis." Equity analysts provide invaluable intelligence on companies' operations and competitive environments. But their task isn't as specialized as attempting to predict next year's top performer out of the 500 large-cap stocks that make up S&P's index. If equity analysts help investors create diversified portfolios of better-than-average performers, they've excelled in their work. So if the market returns –10% and the analysts' picks average –9%, they've done a bang-up job, for professional money managers' needs.

This isn't by any means to knock the idea of creating a diversified portfolio of index-beating stocks. That's the right sort of objective you should set for all but a tiny percentage of the money you choose to self-manage through a process of selecting individual stocks. It'll serve you well in building your wealth over the long run. Trying to find the next #1 is something to do with a very small slice of your portfolio. It can serve as an outlet for your competitive drive or as an enjoyable way to gain valuable knowledge about sizing up companies' prospects.

Some stocks closely resemble past #1s in offering huge upside—provided a few things break the right way. But there's also a significant chance that the most important things will break the wrong way. If that happens, you'll be glad you didn't stash a big chunk of your net worth in your pick for #1, even though you based your selection on lots of diligent analysis.

To understand better why brokerage houses' equity research alone won't lead you to the #1 stock, let's consider one of the analysts' key outputs—price target (PT). Several sources give 12 months as the time frame typically envisioned by PTs. An 18-month period sometimes pops up in those discussions, but let's proceed on the premise that a PT as of December 31 is where the analyst expects the stock to be one year later.

The following case study is based on the first of the five #1 stocks examined in detail in Chapter Two, "These Are Their Stories." It doesn't provide encouragement for relying on the simple expedient of checking out analysts' PTs. At the end of 2016, Bloomberg reported recommendations on NRG Energy's shares by 15 analysts. Twelve of them provided price targets, ranging from $11 to $22. If the most optimistic PT had turned out to be exactly equivalent to the actual price at the end of 2017, NRG's total return for the year would have been 80.5%. The actual total return was 134%. (Total return takes into account not only price change, but also dividends and dividend reinvestment.)

A forecast of an 80.5% total return would have just barely indicated a stock of the caliber associated with #1 ranking. The lowest total return among the 10 stocks that led the S&P 500 between 2012 and 2021 was AMD's 80% in 2018. Next lowest in the group was Southwest Airlines' 126% in 2014. (For a full listing, see the Preface.) Note that even in the two years in which the price of the S&P 500 as a whole declined, 2015 and 2018, the index's best stock more than doubled in price. It's true that in 2008, when the S&P 500 fell by 38.5%, its biggest year-over-year percentage decline since 1937, the year's #1 stock, Family Dollar Stores, produced a total return of just 38%. But in a normal year a start-of-the-year PT that implies a total return of only 80.5%, as in the NRG example, doesn't really tap a stock as a possible #1 performer.

Failing to predict that a stock will double in price is hardly a disgrace. That kind of appreciation results from unforeseen, possibly unforeseeable events. When those events occur, equity analysts raise their PTs to catch up with where the stock has gone.

There's nothing wrong with revising an opinion when the facts change. For example, suppose a stock rises because a setback at a key competitor creates an unforeseen opportunity to pick up market share. The resulting increase in the company's projected free cash flow certainly justifies scrapping the previous PT.

But if the facts don't change, then in principle neither should the analyst's EPS estimate or chosen PE multiple. If the company's prospects don't improve and the overall market's PE doesn't rise, the analyst's PT should remain right where it was, even if the stock's actual price has passed it on the way up. According to the analyst's calculations, the facts indicate that the stock is now trading above fair value. Raising the PT under those circumstances rightly exposes the analyst to the criticism of being concerned mainly about appearing to be behind the curve, rather than with giving investors sound advice. In any case, a start-of-the-year PT that bullishly implies a 12-month gain of 50% or 75% doesn't point to the kind of advance that it ordinarily takes to reach #1.

Remember, too, that the analyst with the highest PT might not be the one among those covering the company who has the best record for picking stocks. In that case, you might be led to think the highest PT is too optimistic, even though it will turn about to be not optimistic enough.

Relying on analysts' consensus view probably won't prove to be the silver bullet, either. Consider this: The top stock among all #1s during 2012–2021, Tesla (2020), began the year with 15 Sell recommendations, against only 11 Buys, according to Bloomberg data.

Faced with the conclusion that fundamental equity research offers no shortcut for picking the top stock, let's move on to examining some alternative approaches. A basic requirement for deeming that a factor is useful in the search for #1 is that the data being employed must be available before the start of the year in which the stock tops the index.

Statistics-Based Selection

Stock Price Volatility

Stocks that trade within a narrow range aren't prime candidates to double in price in the space of 365 days. That would be the financial equivalent of a leopard changing its spots. On the other hand, a stock that bounces wildly up and down might just have an especially high bounce in the coming year. The corollary is that the stock could also drop hugely and underperform the index instead of topping it. That's a good reason to limit your shot at owning the #1 S&P 500 stock to a very small percentage of your portfolio.

Figure 4.1 Previous Year #1 versus #250 Stock Volatility
Source: Bloomberg.

I translated the concept of huge bounces into the numbers illustrated in Figure 4.1. The necessary calculations, which I got from a Bloomberg terminal, can also be run for future years on Excel, once you input the stocks' price histories. To measure volatility, I collected each daily price for the year preceding the stock's reign as #1. I calculated the simple average, also known as the *mean*, of those prices. In addition, I obtained the *standard deviation*, a basic component of a statistician's tool kit that's available on Excel. I divided the standard deviation by the mean and plotted it year-by-year with the graph's solid line. The solid line tracks the comparable measure for each year's #250 stock. You can see that in each case, the #1 stock was more volatile than the #250 stock.

To help you apply this selection device, I next divided each year's #1 volatility number by the corresponding #250 number. That produced a ratio that you can use to eliminate from consideration any stock that's too steady-as-it-goes to have much chance of delivering anything like a 100% gain for the year. From 2012 to 2021, this volatility ratio varied from a low of 1.5 times for Nvidia, which led the S&P 500 in 2016, to a high of 6.3 times for Advanced Micro Devices, the top stock in 2019. In five cases, the ratio was in a range of 1.5 to 1.9 times. In any event, stocks with ratios of less than 1.5 times are not good candidates to win the gold medal.

Sharp-eyed readers who have some experience with these kinds of numbers will point out that AMD was the period's one back-to-back champion stock, ranking #1 in both 2018 and 2019. If a stock goes way up in its first year at the top, it'll register high volatility by my calculation, even if its rise is a straight line rather than a sawtooth pattern. But even though my ratio is intended to capture large up-and-down swings, it turns out not to be a problem in AMD's case. In 2018, the stock led the pack even though its price plunged by 49% between September 14 and December 24. So even though AMD was 2018's #1, it entered its second index-leading year, 2019, as a stock that still met the standard of being subject to both huge spikes and steep declines.

Dispersion in EPS Forecasts

If the statistical term "dispersion" isn't familiar to you, don't fear that you're about to confront a page full of Greek letters and mathematical equations. In quant-speak the word just refers to how spread out a set of numbers is. The numbers we're talking about here are equity analysts' EPS estimates.

Yes, I know. All along I've been downplaying the relevance of equity analysts' outputs to the hunt for #1. But here's the difference. Those dismissive comments dealt with what analysts were consciously trying to achieve by generating recommendations, earnings estimates, and price targets. This discussion, in contrast, involves something the analysts never had in mind, but accomplished nevertheless. And their genuinely useful contribution had nothing to do with which particular analyst did the best job in the assigned task. The most wildly wrong forecast was as important to the process as the one that came closest to the mark.

It turns out that a high level of dispersion among beginning-of-year EPS estimates is a common trait of the #1 stocks. I've quantified this effect with the newly hatched "Fridson-Lee Statistic." To calculate it, I take a #1 stock's highest EPS estimate, as of the end of the year prior to its index-topping performance. From that number I subtract the lowest estimate. Then I divide that difference by the lowest estimate and express the result as a percentage. Here's a hypothetical example:

Highest EPS estimate:	*$2.40*
Lowest EPS estimate:	*$1.80*
Fridson-Lee Statistic:	*($2.40 – $1.80) ÷ ($1.80)*
	= $0.60 ÷ $1.80
	= 0.333
	= 33.3%

For comparison, I calculate the Fridson-Lee Statistic for the middle-of-the-pack stock, the one that finished at #250 in the year that the stock in question was #1 (see Table 4.1). The last column in the table displays the percentage difference between the #1 stock and the #250 stock.

In all 10 years, the #1 stock had greater dispersion in its EPS estimates than the #250 stock. The median difference was 33.9 percentage points. Two of the #1 stocks' Fridson-Lee Statistics exceeded the middle-of-the-pack stock's by almost 200 percentage points.

What do these numbers tell us? If all the analysts' EPS estimates for a stock are tightly bunched together, as in the table's middle column, it means there's close to a unanimous opinion about the company's likely operating performance for the coming year. That kind of stock probably isn't going to surprise investors on either the upside or the downside.

Table 4.1 Fridson-Lee Statistic (%)

| | Analysts' EPS Estimates | | |
| | #1 Stock | Prior-Year #250 Stock | |
Year	High-Low/Low	High-Low/Low	Difference
2012	44.4%	7.3%	37.2%
2013	69.6%	2.2%	67.3%
2014	33.6%	2.9%	30.6%
2015	68.8%	3.2%	65.6%
2016	18.4%	3.7%	14.7%
2017	195.7%	1.9%	193.8%
2018	23.3%	2.2%	21.0%
2019	19.0%	4.0%	14.9%
2020	197.0%	2.2%	194.8%
2021	11.7%	2.2%	9.5%
Median	39.0%	2.6%	33.9%

Source: Bloomberg.

Everything important that's going to happen to the company is baked into its stock price when the year begins. Most likely, the stock will perform roughly in line with the market.

To break out of the pack, a company has to surprise a portion of the active investors who determine where its stock trades. For a #1 stock, the investors who get surprised are the ones who shared the pessimistic view of the analysts with the lowest EPS estimates. And as you may have been about to say, a stock with a high Fridson-Lee statistic also has the potential to surprise the investors who thought the analysts with the highest EPS estimates were more in the ballpark. In that case, the stock will probably end up ranking somewhere near the bottom of the S&P 500. That's the challenge—some might say the fun—of aiming to buy a stock before it zooms to the top of the index.

The key takeaway: When you survey the S&P 500 for a candidate to reach #1, eliminate from consideration stocks on which there's anything resembling unanimity in analysts' EPS estimates. Those stocks are likely to meet investors' expectations, no more and no less. That's a formula for middling performance. In 90% of the cases we examined, the Fridson-Lee statistic just prior to takeoff was 18% or higher, with some stocks clocking in at nearly 200%. Those numbers identify the territory where you have the best chance of finding #1.

Bond Ratings

This statistical measure may seem out of place in a discussion of stock-picking. Only once during my Wall Street years did I ever hear an equity research manager refer to bond ratings. At that time, the U.S. economy was clearly heading into a recession. Figuring that companies would need to be in strong financial condition to weather the downturn, the equity research director ordered his analysts to restrict their Buy recommendations to companies with investment-grade ratings. That category ranges from Aaa to Baa3 at Moody's and from AAA to BBB– at Standard & Poor's. (A third major agency, Fitch Ratings, uses the same scale as Standard & Poor's.)

The investment-grade category currently features some of America's most celebrated companies. Alphabet, Amazon, Apple, Meta Platforms, Microsoft, and Walmart regularly pop up prominently in the financial media. Where their stocks don't show up is in the #1 slot in the S&P 500. Those six super-famous companies accounted for just one of the 50 top-five stocks of 2012–2021. (Amazon claimed the #2 spot in 2015.)

Only one of the 10 companies that did make it to #1 in the 10-year period began its top-of-the-chart year with an investment-grade rating. And that company was rated just one step above speculative-grade ("junk" in the media's favored phrase). Southwest Airlines stood at Baa3 by Moody's (Figure 4.2) and BBB– by Standard & Poor's (Figure 4.3) at the start of 2014. Five of the 10 index leaders weren't rated at all by Moody's.

These numbers tell us that if you're trying to figure out which S&P 500 stock will deliver the highest total return in the coming year, you should focus your search where the credit ratings record says you're most likely to find the winner. Stick to below-investment grade companies or, at most, those that are rated just one notch higher than that.

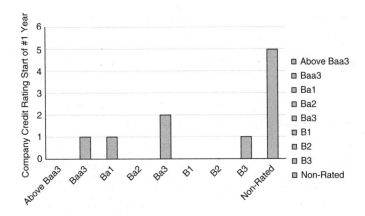

Figure 4.2 Company Credit Ratings at Start of #1 Year (2012–2021), Moody's

Source: Bloomberg.

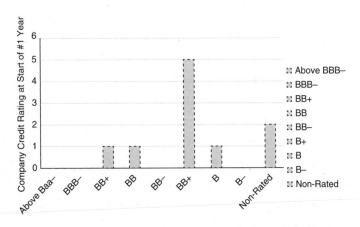

Figure 4.3 Company Credit Ratings at Start of #1 Year (2012–2021), Standard & Poor's

Source: Bloomberg.

If anything, consider the lack of a Moody's rating a favorable sign. Equity analysts may not pay a lot of attention to bond ratings, but you should if you're searching for #1.

On a technical point, the accompanying bar graphs are based on the letter grades variously called "Long-Term Corporate Family Rating" or "Long-Term Local Issuer Credit." Those ratings are typically applied to companies' senior unsecured bonds. Senior secured bonds will generally be rated a bit higher and subordinated bonds a bit lower than the company rating.

Note, too, that if there's a Moody's rating it may not exactly match the corresponding Standard & Poor's rating. For example, Moody's Ba3 corresponds to Standard & Poor's BB–. So if a company has one of those ratings but not the other, it's called a "split-rated" credit. If that situation arises, you can classify the company's rating as the midpoint between the two.

But can you really feel comfortable owning the stock of a company with a bond rating that journalists routinely refer to as "junk?" Yes, you can. A below-investment-grade rating does typically reflect a balance sheet with a fairly hefty debt load. But small size and a high level of business uncertainty also contribute to placing a company in speculative-grade territory. As discussed elsewhere in this chapter, those traits can actually be favorable signs for future #1 status.

Contrary to the impression created by the derogatory "junk" label, a bond rating below Baa3/BBB– doesn't automatically signify a failing company. The speculative-grade category does include some "fallen angels." Those are companies that formerly carried investment-grade ratings but have suffered a decline. Some of them continue deteriorating until they default on their debt and file for bankruptcy. But that doesn't describe the companies explored in these pages. In fact, half of them have earned the designation "rising star," receiving upgrades to investment-grade either during or after their reigns as #1 stock performers. By 2022, AMD had ascended to A– and Nvidia had climbed all the way to A at Standard & Poor's. The "Qualitative Considerations" section below offers some hints on spotting the sort of improving credit trend that helped those rising stars excel during their best-in-class years.

Market Capitalization

The final statistical selection factor doesn't have a flawless record, but, even so, using it should improve your chances of picking the right candidate for the #1 slot. In general, the companies that achieve that distinction aren't among the biggest-market-value, most-talked-about ones. You'll usually do best to focus on stocks with a smaller market capitalization (share price times number of shares outstanding) than

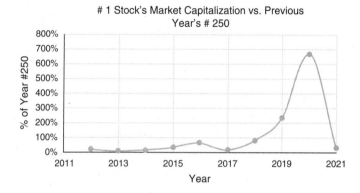

Figure 4.4 #1 Stock's Market Capitalization vs. Previous Year's #250
Source: Bloomberg.

the previous year's middle-of-the-pack stock (#250). (See Figure 4.4.)

Half of the stocks had a start-of-the-year market cap less than one-third that of the previous year's #250 stock's market cap. The median ratio was 33.5%. Netflix (2015) scored the lowest by this measure, at just 5%. Aside from the two exceptions discussed in the next paragraph, the highest ratio was 80%, for Advanced Micro Devices in 2018. The odds favor focusing your search on stocks with ratios at or below that threshold.

The most spectacular exception to the finding that #1 stocks generally have smaller market caps than middle-of-the-pack performers is 2020's winner, Tesla. That company is unlike most #1 stocks in other important ways. Not only is its index-leading total return by far the highest in the group at 743%, but the volatility graph above shows that it was also an outlier by that measure. And it had more of a celebrity status than its peers, thanks in no small part to its colorful CEO, Elon Musk. In my judgment, it would be a mistake to reject market cap as a selection factor based on the ratio associated with such an unrepresentative member of the #1 club.

True, there was a second exception to the rule of blue-ribbon winners coming from the ranks of stocks with market caps of 80% or less than the market cap of the previous year's 250th-ranked stock. Advanced Micro Devices had a 236% ratio when it began its 2019 reign at the top of the S&P 500. But that was after leading the pack in 2018, when it began the year at 80% of the market cap of 2017's #250. Just as TSLA is dissimilar to the other #10 stocks in important ways, AMD is atypical in being the group's only back-to-back winner. Perhaps you should give market cap less weight than the other statistical measures as you attempt to zero in on your one pick for the coming year's #1. But you shouldn't reject it simply because AMD was an exception in one of its two championship years.

Rejected Statistical Selection Methods

Just as it's important to know what works in identifying top stocks, it's important to know what doesn't work. It might seem natural, after years of following brokerage houses' equity research, to assume that that the qualities they use to describe "good" companies are the keys to index-leading performance. In addition, you can probably think of other characteristics that seem like obvious requirements for delivering excellent returns. And then there are things that "everybody knows" about why stocks behave as they do.

Possibly the most important point to take away from this book is that nothing about the top stocks is self-evident. Every conceivable clue is in the realm of supposition unless and until it's validated with hard facts. Conducting your search for #1 on the basis of unproven assertions will lead you down highly unproductive paths.

In my years as a Wall Street corporate bond research director I devoted time to debunking a large portion of what I'd been taught in my earlier years as a trader.

- "Everybody knew" that when a bond got downgraded from investment-grade, the vast majority of investors shunned it due to the stigma of a "junk" rating. Those bonds invariably traded below their intrinsic value, leaving easy opportunities for smarter players to earn superior returns.
- "Everybody knew" that when a company cut its dividend, it left more cash available to service its debt. So the company's bonds subsequently outperformed their peers.

- "Everybody knew" that the higher the yield on Treasury bonds, the greater is the yield differential between speculative-grade bonds and Treasury bonds.

When I tested these ideas with actual market data, it turned out that what "everybody knew" was wrong in every single case.

As a result of conducting this research I realized that a lot of what I'd been told in the trenches was made up by bond salesmen. Their job was to persuade portfolio managers to buy whatever was in their traders' inventory. The salesmen could get the trades done and earn their commission by relying on market lore that had never been subjected to rigorous, evidence-based testing. It made no difference if one statement about how the market supposedly worked actually contradicted another, meaning that the two statements couldn't both be true.

Anyone who dared to question the time-honored lore could usually be kept in line with an insinuation that doing so was a sign of inexperience. Another ploy was to cite an anecdotal example that upheld the common wisdom. That proved nothing, of course, because there could have been—and generally were—many more examples that contradicted what "everybody knew."

This gets us into the area of trading rules. The concept is to buy (or sell) whenever certain conditions are satisfied. No trading rule is expected to produce a profit every single time. It's valid if it succeeds significantly more often than not, producing an above-market return over time.

I've noticed that some purported experts promulgate trading rules but skip the step of demonstrating statistically that they work. If they were ever challenged on that matter, they'd probably "explain" that trading is an art, not a science. They'd then boast about their "feel for the market."

Getting back to my research on corporate bond market lore, I'm pleased to say my findings were well received by our institutional customers. But I expected them to have no impact on our own traders—and I wasn't disappointed. The head of one trading desk actually told me, with regard to his team, "We are not seekers of truth." He was right. That wasn't part of their job description. Generating profits was. The only question was whether the customers could succeed by heeding the advice of the traders and salespeople.

In fairness, I found that some salespeople had a way to protect their customers from bad purchases without incurring the traders' wrath. They'd present the proposed trade, just as they were expected to, but they'd convey their lack of enthusiasm through the tone of their voice. This strategy sacrificed an immediate sales commission. But it helped build a loyal customer relationship, which was more valuable to the salesperson over the long run.

Here's the point of this digression that relates to trying to find #1 stocks: There are lots of plausible guesses about what distinguishes them from the rest of the pile. But they're just that—guesses—unless someone crunches the numbers to determine whether they actually work.

The statistics-based selection criteria listed above are the ones that do in fact work. They're the keepers among numerous possibilities that I tested with John Lee's help. Before we ran our tests, all of them seemed like they might be useful in narrowing down the list of candidates for #1 stock. But only a few panned out. By examining the following list of rejected screening methods, you can save yourself going down some blind alleys.

I tested each item not just on the #1 stocks, but on the S&P 500's five best-performing stock for each year. Expanding the number of stocks in the test made the results more reliable. Each item in the list includes a hypothesis—the effect that I thought I might find—and what I actually found. In every case, the data source is Bloomberg.

Analyst-Predicted Percentage Price Gain

Traditional equity analysis generates price targets. Comparing a stock's current price with its price target generates a predicted percentage price gain. An investor might reasonably infer that if the analysts in aggregate possess wisdom about their companies' prospects, then the best stocks to own are the ones with the highest consensus predicted percentage price gains.

Hypothesis   The top five stocks began their top-five-ranking years with higher predicted percentage price gains than the bottom 495 stocks.

Finding   There was no discernible pattern of stocks that ranked in the top five having larger expected percentage price gains than the bottom 495 stocks.

Average Five-Year Revenue Growth

Traditional equity analysis often highlights strong past performance, measured in various ways, as part of the case for buying a stock.

Hypothesis   The top five stocks had higher average revenue growth during the five years prior to ranking in the top five than the bottom 495.

Finding   There was no discernible pattern of the top five stocks having higher average revenue growth than the bottom 495.

Average Growth in Return on Equity

Traditional securities analysis attributes great significance to return on equity (ROE), defined as Net Income divided by Shareholders' Equity, expressed as a percentage. (The denominator is the average of the beginning-of-year and end-of-year Shareholders' Equity.) An especially strong trend of improvement in this profitability measure might be a sign that a stock is about to zoom to the performance table's top percentile.

Hypothesis   Top-five stocks exhibit higher average annual growth in ROE than other stocks in the five years prior to being ranked among the S&P 500's five highest total return stocks.

Finding   There was no discernible tendency of top-five stocks to outdo the other 495 in terms of average growth in ROE in the five years preceding their outstanding returns.

Average Free Cash Flow Yield

This book refers in several places to the importance of free cash flow (FCF), rather than earnings per share, in determining stock valuations. FCF is defined as Cash Flow from Operations − Capital Expenditures. One might guess that top-five companies display higher Free Cash Flow Yields than less-performing ones. The FCF yield is defined as Free Cash Flow per Share divided by Current Share Price, expressed as a percentage.

Hypothesis   Top-five stocks have higher average FCF yields than other stocks at the end of the year prior to their top-five performance.

Finding   There was no pattern of higher FCF yields on top-five stocks than on bottom-495 stocks.

Short Interest

In the event of a positive surprise in operating performance, a heavily shorted stock may receive an extra boost from short-sellers who are scrambling to cover their shorts. This raises the possibility that the highest returns are delivered by the stocks with the highest *short interest ratios* at the beginning of the period. This measure is defined as the number of shares sold short divided by the stock's average daily trading volume.

Hypothesis   At the end of the year prior year to ranking in the highest 1%, top-five stocks had higher short interest ratios than the bottom 495 stocks.

Finding There was no identifiable pattern of top-five stocks beginning their great years with higher short interest ratios than the bottom 495 stocks.

Insider Buying

Publicly traded corporations report purchases and sales of their shares by their directors, officers, and executives. Purchases by these insiders are commonly interpreted as signs that the individuals with the best handle on their company's prospects believe its stock is undervalued. It might seem to follow that the index-topping performance is usually preceded by a high level of insider buying.

Hypothesis Top-five stocks consistently had higher levels of insider buying in the year preceding their rankings in the highest 1% than other S&P 500 stocks.

Finding There was no evidence of higher levels of insider buying among top-five stocks than among other stocks.

Rating Agency Outlooks

In addition to rating companies' bonds, Moody's and Standard & Poor's publish outlooks for their ratings. They indicate the likely future direction of a company's rating as Positive, Stable, or Negative. As discussed later in "Quantitative Considerations," some of the #1 stocks showed signs of improving credit quality before they began their index-topping years. Can this favorable factor be documented with the use of rating outlooks?

Hypothesis   There was a consistent pattern of top-five companies having Positive rating outlooks as of the end of the year preceding their reigns as index leaders.

Finding   The top-five companies' rating outlooks showed no consistent pattern, either Positive or Negative.

Why Didn't These Plausible Selection Methods Work?

The preceding discussion of rejected statistical selection methods mentions some stalwarts of standard equity analysis, namely, revenue growth and return on equity. Also among the rejects is a measure based on free cash flow, which this book has showcased as superior to mainstream stock analysts' focus, earnings per share. Analysts' price targets haven't done a stellar job of distinguishing the top-1% champions from the bottom-99% also-rans. Indicators drawn from market data, short interest, and insider buying haven't panned out, either. And even though we found that bond ratings differentiated #1 stocks from the pack, and detail below how improving ratings helped vault some companies to the top spot in the S&P 500, the rating agencies' own rating outlooks weren't especially helpful in spotting the next blue-ribbon winner. These proposed indicators make intuitive sense. Why don't they turn out to help in the search for #1?

It comes back to the element of surprise. The stock market does a pretty good job of reflecting what's already known about a stock. You don't have to believe that the market is perfectly "efficient," in academic parlance, to recognize that it's no easy feat to beat the averages using information that's already available to everybody who's trying to get an edge. Quant shops that try to predict future price moves with sophisticated algorithms employ armies of PhDs and still don't always get it right.

When stockbrokers recommend a stock on the grounds that it has a proven record of high profits, first-class management, and a strong balance sheet, they're generally talking about things that were also true last year and the year before. If the pitch includes the claim that the market has inexplicably ignored all these virtues, but sooner or later investors will come to realize what a gem the company is, you can feel perfectly comfortable ignoring the recommendation and moving on to the next idea. Unless the company's operations suddenly start to perform better than anticipated, there's no reason why the market should spontaneously start assigning a higher relative valuation to its stock.

Consider the history of Zoom Video Communications (ZM). This company, not an S&P 500 member as of 2022, provides an online platform that enables people at different physical locations to meet by video. The company went public in April 2019 amid hopes that demand for its services would grow over time as remote work became more common.

No one was expecting what happened not long afterwards. On January 9, 2020, the World Health Organization reported a mysterious coronavirus-related pneumonia in Wuhan, China. It soon became clear that, in response to the COVID-19 pandemic, offices would shut down. Working from home, employees would need to meet remotely. In the first two months of 2020 Zoom acquired more new users than in all of 2019. By mid-April ZM had doubled from its previous year-end level, and in 2020 as a whole the price nearly quadrupled.

Admittedly, this is an extreme example. But it makes the point: Stocks don't rack up monster-sized gains as a result of investors finally registering information that's long since been available. It requires something unexpected to happen.

The triggering event doesn't necessarily have to be something that was *totally* unexpected, as it was in Zoom's case. It's sufficient for positive shock to be unexpected by a substantial portion of the investors whose collective judgment sets the stock's price. That's why one of the many selection methods that I tested, dispersion in EPS forecasts, does work.

When everyone involved in the stock has essentially the same view of the company's outlook, their best-case outcome isn't much different from their worst-case outcome. If it then becomes clear that the best-case outcome will turn out to be the actual outcome, nobody is going to get very excited about it. But if half the investors previously thought the company was going down the tubes, the modest earnings improvement that the other half expected will shift the naysayers' perceptions, and the stock will rally.

Up to this point, I've pinned down the concrete, measurable factors that can help you narrow the field of potential full-year pacesetters. I've also spared you going down some false paths in the use of facts and figures that are available before the start of a stock's banner year. The rest the process of naming your pick for #1 will involve qualitative judgments. To assist in that part of the challenge, I'll extract from the narratives presented in Chapter Two, "These Are Their Stories," and Chapter Three, "News Flash! There Are More Than 500 Stocks in the World," certain developments that contributed to stocks' #1 years. Then I'll discuss some characteristics—not ones that can absolutely be reduced to numbers—that may help steer you to the best in class among your leading candidates.

Qualitative Considerations

Outside Pressure for Change

In 2017 NRG went from a laggard to a pacesetter by a fundamental shift in strategy. The company abandoned its ambition to become a leader in renewable energy in favor of safer, steadier profits in more traditional forms of power generation. Activist investors Paul Singer and C. John Wilder were instrumental in bringing about this transformation. But signs of change were already visible before the year began. The CEO architect of the green strategy had been fired in December 2015. Wind and solar operations were scaled back in 2016, and NRG cut its dividend to facilitate increased investment in conventional power.

In ETSY's case, several activist investors arrived on the scene in 2017, the year before it beat all S&P 500 stocks. They took large positions in ETSY and pushed for a shift in strategy. The company brought in Goldman Sachs to undertake a strategic review, and takeover speculation ensued. Soon Etsy had a new CEO, chief financial officer, and chief technology officer. Cost-cutting was in, and the culture of relying exclusively on in-house engineering was out.

Before Devon Energy began its index-leading year, 2020, management had set the stage by selling low-yielding properties with long paybacks. That provided more cash to invest in shale oil prospects with greater near-term potential. The strategic overhaul played into what investors were looking for at the time—higher returns on equity in the short term. Devon was also recognized as being at the industry's forefront in adopting innovative, highly efficient drilling technologies.

Dynamic Technology

Stocks don't double in a year without some major change in their circumstances. The change can involve their business prospects, and it could happen to any company, for a variety of reasons. But rapidly evolving technology increases the chances.

The semiconductor business is characterized by short product life-cycles. Competitors pursue diverse solutions in the efforts to seize the lead in the next phase of development. Investors can't be certain which approach will succeed. But a stock that checks other boxes as a possible #1 has an additional shot at the top if it operates in this kind of business setting.

Advanced Micro Devices thrived in such an environment during 2019. The company made substantial headway in the server, central processing unit, and graphics-processing unit segments. Market sources reported that Advanced Micro was also poised to make inroads in the personal computer and data center markets.

Also in 2019, ENPH a non-S&P 500 stock at the time, posted three times as high a total return as index-leader AMD. Enphase's successes in the technologically dynamic solar equipment business were a key to that spectacular result. The company's eighth-generation IQ line leap-frogged competitors by operating without batteries, which made it the low-cost option.

Among other companies examined in the preceding chapters, SolarEdge Technologies, Tesla, and Devon Energy were also recognized as technology leaders in their industries. That trait isn't guaranteed to deliver a world-changing breakthrough every single year. And it's not as easily quantifiable as stock price volatility or dispersion in EPS forecasts. But technological leadership is definitely a qualitative consideration that can put a company in contention for the #1 slot.

Signs of Potential Credit Quality Improvement

Credit quality improvement played a role in the vanquishing of all S&P 500 stocks by NRG and Enphase. NRG's credit quality improvement was acknowledged in its stellar year of 2017 by a Moody's upgrade of its rating outlook from Stable to Positive. Enphase demonstrated its improved financial strength by announcing, early in its year of outpacing all 500 S&P stocks (2019), that it had paid off its term loan in full.

One other company's story prominently featured credit quality improvement. Both Moody's and Standard & Poor's raised their bond ratings on Advanced Micro Devices in 2017. Those upgrades, though, were old news and presumably fully priced into AMD by the time it began its 2018 reign as #1. The company's financial profile continued to improve, though, with Standard & Poor's delivering another upgrade in 2019.

As noted in "Rejected Statistical Selection Methods," positive bond rating outlooks aren't surefire guides to identifying #1 stocks ahead of time. But if you look closely into your candidate companies' finances, you may discover some hints of credit quality improvement to come. For instance, analysts were already commenting on NRG's strong balance sheet in 2016, the year before it topped the S&P 500.

On the face of it, that positive characteristic was in the category of things already known about the company. As I've stressed, outsized stock returns come about because something changes. In that connection, research by Robert W. Holthausen and Richard W. Leftwich published in 1986[1] found that stock prices respond favorably to upgrades of bond rating outlooks, as enjoyed by NRG in the course of its #1 year, although not to upgrades of the ratings themselves. And it's not the rating outlook that matters but a change in the rating outlook.

It may be possible to get ahead of the upgrades in outlook by closely studying a candidate company's financial statements. While it's not true, as their critics maintain, that the rating agencies analyze companies through the rearview mirror, they do seek clear confirmation of a trend before revising their opinions. By doing so, they avoid frequent upgrades and downgrades in response to short-term ups and downs in a company's fortunes.

The rating agencies could make their ratings jump around more frenetically if that's what bondholders desired. But, in fact, managers of debt portfolios generally urge the rating agencies to maintain a longer-term focus. Otherwise, the debt managers might be compelled to sell out of a downgraded company's bonds in order to maintain their intended ratings mix. Then they'd reenter the name when it climbed back to its previous rating a short time later. Making that sort of round trip is much costlier than staying put throughout the dip and the rebound. Many corporate bonds are comparatively illiquid, so in-and-out trading imposes heavy transaction costs that detract from portfolio managers' performance.

Financial ratios are a significant part of the bond rating process, although more subjective factors also play a role. Rating agencies and credit analysts have devised many variants of ratios that measure profit margins, return on capital, debt leverage, and interest coverage. For example, my book

Table 4.2 Ratios for Use in Spotting Improving Credit Trends

$$\frac{\text{Sales} - \text{Cost of Goods Sold}}{\text{Sales}}$$

$$\frac{\text{Net Income} - \text{Dividends}}{\text{Total Debt} + \text{Total Equity}}$$

$$\frac{\text{Total Debt}}{\text{EBITDA}}$$

$$\frac{\text{EBITDA}}{\text{Interest Expense}}$$

EBITDA = Earnings Before Interest, Taxes, Depreciation, and Amortization
Total Debt = Long-Term Debt + Short-Term Debt + Current Maturities of Long-Term Debt
For Total Debt/EBITDA, a declining trend over time indicates improving credit quality. For the others, improving credit quality is indicated by a rising trend.

(co-authored by Fernando Alvarez) *Financial Statement Analysis: A Practitioner's Guide* (Fifth Edition, 2022) lists several that Fitch Ratings provided for the chapter on credit analysis. But you can potentially pick up a trend of improving credit quality by calculating the simple ratios described in Table 4.2 for each of the past few years.

Favorable trends in these measures of credit quality over the past few years can be taken as a favorable qualitative factor in your quest to spot next year's #1 stock. This analysis may enable you get ahead of an upgrade in a credit agency's rating outlook, which research has shown to be associated with an increase in the stock price. But even if that doesn't happen, finding that a company's credit profile is improving will confirm that it resembles some of those that have topped the S&P 500 standings in the past. Keep in mind, though, that the improvement is from a level that consigns the company to a borderline or actual speculative-grade ("junk" in financial media talk) bond rating.

Dominant Competitor

Three of the companies highlighted in these pages were long constrained by being pitted against gargantuan competitors. That predicament can actually turn out to be a favorable characteristic when it comes to finding the prize stock among the potential gold medalists. Breaking out of the competitive bind, through either innovation or faltering by the industry's Goliath, can help thrust a company to the top.

Etsy faced Amazon, the most formidable rival-crusher of them all. But before the start of 2018, the year in which the much smaller e-tailer beat all the S&P 500 members' stock returns from outside their ranks, avid equity research followers knew that Etsy had rearranged the competitive landscape. Loop Capital's Blake Harper proclaimed that the company's investments in artificial intelligence had enabled it to counter Amazon's stepped-up efforts in Etsy's niche. This was a good example of the value that stock analysts provide in explaining industry dynamics.

Incursion into a company's product area by a much bigger competitor was also a problem faced by Enphase Energy prior to its 2019 takeoff. Huawei Technologies, which already dominated utility-scale solar projects, started shipping to the residential market, where Enphase concentrated its efforts. That new threat was a drag on ETSY's price until fate took a hand. Huawei's chief financial officer was arrested on suspicion of violating U.S. trade sanctions on Iran. That event dealt a setback to the Chinese giant's efforts.

Advanced Micro Devices similarly benefited in 2018 when an industry heavyweight appeared to falter. Its shares rose following a report that a flaw in certain Intel chips exposed operating systems using them to hacking. AMD rose despite *Barron's* backing up of Intel's statement that the chips contained no such flaw. This all took place against a backdrop of some major chip customers wanting to reduce their reliance on Intel.

Underdogs don't always catch breaks that enable them to pick up market share or fend off encroachments by more powerful competitors. But as the stories of the #1 stocks show, something major has to change in order for a company to rise to the top. Being under the heel of an industry colossus at least creates the potential for a significant shift in the marketplace dynamics.

Postscript to a Very Bad Year

The preceding exploration of tip-offs to the top stocks, all but one of which returned more than 100%, is based on the years 2012–2021. That period included two down years for the level of the S&P 500, but not the truly horrendous downturn triggered by the Global Financial Crisis a few years earlier. The #1 stock of 2008, Family Dollar Stores (FDO), returned only 36%. But the statistical selection factors that held in the better years also applied in the stock market's worst year since the Great Depression.

FDO was 3.85 times as volatile in 2007 as that year's #250 stock, well above the minimum recommended 1.5 times ratio. As for dispersion in price targets, FDO's Fridson-Lee Statistic, at 16%, was only a bit below the 18% threshold that typified #1 stocks during 2012–2021 and higher than the 11.7% level of the one #1 stock that was below that threshold. The company wasn't rated by the credit agencies in 2008. But its initial ratings by Moody's (Ba2 in 2015) and Standard & Poor's (BBB– in 2011) strongly suggest that the company's credit quality was speculative-grade, or at most one step above, when it led the S&P 500. Finally, at the end of 2007 FDO had 43% of the market cap of that year's #250 stock. That was not far from the 33.5% median for that statistic.

Based on these results, the statistical guidelines that emerged from the companies chronicled in these pages should apply well, come rain or come shine, in the years ahead.

Chapter Five

Begin Your Assault
on the Summit!

—— ❧ ——

Are you ready to satisfy that speculative urge so that it doesn't infect the primary objective of investing prudently for your children's education and your retirement?

Perhaps you like to talk about stocks with your friends and crow about the ones that worked out profitably for you. If so, you and your pals might want to create a pool on next year's #1 S&P 500 stock. Or maybe your motivation is that you just enjoy matching your wits against the market.

Whatever form your investment thrill-seeking takes, trying to pick the top performer can be a fairly harmless outlet. Provided, that is, you don't commit more than a couple of percentage points of your portfolio to the effort. Meanwhile, the research you devote to the quest can pay solid dividends in the form of learning about what makes stocks excel.

Gaining a fuller understanding of the market isn't the only way you can come out a winner, even if you don't succeed in picking the top stock. If your choice ends up "only" finishing in the top five, you'll probably still be a pretty happy camper. Between 2012 and 2021, the #5 stock in the S&P 500 delivered a total return in the range of 57% to 141%.

Heck, even landing in the top tenth of the index isn't too shabby. Returns on the #50 stock ranged from 20% to 71%. And that worst outcome, 20% in 2018, was a home run in the context of a −8% return on the S&P 500 as a whole.

So if you go through all the steps summarized below and still can't narrow your choice down to one, there's nothing wrong with splitting the allocation among two or three stocks. Together, though, they should still not total more than a couple of percentage points of your total portfolio value. And if you're in some kind of competition to pick the top stock, you'll have to go with the one that feels the most right for that purpose.

You just have to keep in mind that the best candidates for #1 are prone to surprises. The surprises come in two flavors. One of them is the negative kind. If you're on the receiving end of that kind of surprise, the stock you picked could wind up near the bottom of the rankings. That's why you shouldn't risk more than a small piece of your portfolio on the idea.

If you're game, here's a recap of the characteristics to look for in making your selection for next year's #1 S&P 500 stock. (See Chapter Four, "Tip-Offs to Top Stocks," for details of the calculations.)

Choose a stock with all of the following quantitative characteristics:

- Price volatility over the previous year at least 1.5 times as great as the stock that ranked #250 by total return.
- Fridson-Lee Statistic (a measure of dispersion in analysts' EPS estimates) of 18% or greater.
- Bond ratings of Baa3 or lower by Moody's and BBB– or lower by Standard & Poor's.
- Market capitalization equivalent to 80% or less of the market capitalization of the stock that ranked #250 by total return in the previous year. (Some #1 stocks have been exceptions to this one.)

Look for one or more of the following qualitative characteristics:

- Outside pressure for change.
- Dynamic technology.
- Signs of potential credit quality improvement (not including bond rating agencies' outlooks).
- Dominant competitor.

At the end of these comments you'll find summaries (Table 5.1) of how the 10 #1 stocks of 2012–2021 stacked up by the quantitative measures. The statistics are as of the day before they took off for the top of the performance rankings.

You now have the blueprint for a different way of viewing stocks than you've read about anywhere else. If you're intrigued by the challenge of picking next year's best-performing S&P 500 stock, these principles will focus your search on the premier candidates. Equity reports from Wall Street and independent research organizations can help you identify companies with the qualitative characteristics that strengthen the case for a stock.

Go forth with the motto *E pluribus unum*: Out of many (500, to be precise), one. After all, why shouldn't you be among the ~~lucky~~ smart investors who own the highest-return stock in the index?

Table 5.1 Statistical Profile of the #1 Stocks of 2012–2021

As of	31-Dec-12
Name	PULTEGROUP INC
Ticker	PHM
Industry	Consumer Discretionary
Volatility as percentage of #250 stock	420.6%
Fridson-Lee Statistic	44.4%
Bond Ratings	
Moody's	Not Rated
Standard & Poor's	BB–
Market capitalization as percentage of #250 S&P 500 stock	20.1%
As of	31-Dec-13
Name	NETFLIX INC
Ticker	NFLX
Industry	Communication Services
Volatility as percentage of #250 stock	231.8%
Fridson-Lee Statistic	69.6%
Bond Ratings	
Moody's	Ba3
Standard & Poor's	BB–
Market capitalization as percentage of #250 S&P 500 stock	49.0%
As of	31-Dec-14
Name	SOUTHWEST AIRLINES CO
Ticker	LUV
Industry	Industrials
Volatility as percentage of #250 stock	175.4%
Fridson-Lee Statistic	33.6%
Bond Ratings	
Moody's	Baa3
Standard & Poor's	BBB–
Market capitalization as percentage of #250 S&P 500 stock	15.3%

(Continued)

Table 5.1 (*continued*)

As of	31-Dec-15
Name	NETFLIX INC
Ticker	NFLX
Industry	Communication Services
Volatility as percentage of #250 stock	185.6%
Fridson-Lee Statistic	68.8%
Bond Ratings	
Moody's	Ba3
Standard & Poor's	BB–
Market capitalization as percentage of #250 S&P 500 stock	34.4%

As of	31-Dec-16
Name	NVIDIA CORP
Ticker	NVDA
Industry	Information Technology
Volatility as percentage of #250 stock	146.5%
Fridson-Lee Statistic	18.4%
Bond Ratings	
Moody's	Not Rated
Standard & Poor's	BB+
Market capitalization as percentage of #250 S&P 500 stock	62.0%

As of	31-Dec-17
Name	NRG ENERGY INC
Ticker	NRG
Industry	Utilities
Volatility as percentage of #250 stock	174.0%
Fridson-Lee Statistic	195.7%
Bond Ratings	
Moody's	Not Rated
Standard & Poor's	BB–
Market capitalization as percentage of #250 S&P 500 stock	16.3%

(Continued)

Table 5.1 (*continued*)

As of	31-Dec-18
Name	ADVANCED MICRO DEVICES
Ticker	AMD
Industry	Information Technology
Volatility as percentage of #250 stock	284.7%
Fridson-Lee Statistic	23.3%
Bond Ratings	
Moody's	Not Rated
Standard & Poor's	B–
Market Capitalization as percentage of #250 S&P 500 stock	80.5%
As of	31-Dec-19
Name	ADVANCED MICRO DEVICES
Ticker	AMD
Industry	Information Technology
Volatility as percentage of #250 stock	626.0%
Fridson-Lee Statistic	19.0%
Bond Ratings	
Moody's	Not Rated
Standard & Poor's	B+
Market capitalization as percentage of #250 S&P 500 stock	236.0%
As of	31-Dec-20
Name	TESLA INC
Ticker	TSLA
Industry	Consumer Discretionary
Volatility as percentage of #250 stock	184.1%
Fridson-Lee Statistic	197.0%
Bond Ratings	
Moody's	B3
Standard & Poor's	B–
Market capitalization as percentage of #250 S&P 500 stock	669.1%

(Continued)

Table 5.1 (*continued*)

As of	31-Dec-21
Name	DEVON ENERGY CORP
Ticker	DVN
Industry	Energy
Volatility as percentage of #250 stock	278.7%
Fridson-Lee Statistic	11.7%
Bond Ratings	
Moody's	Ba1
Standard & Poor's	BB–
Market capitalization as percent of #250 S&P 500 stock	32.5%

Notes

⁓

Preface

1. Erin Gobler. "Stonks, Apes, YOLO: Your Guide to Meme Stock Trading Slang." The Balance. Updated 19 June 2022. Online version https://www.thebalancemoney.com/your-guide-to-meme-stock-trading-slang-5216722

2. Vildana Hajiric and Michael P. Regan. "Jeremy Siegel Says It's OK to 'Gamble' on Speculative Stocks." Bloomberg News. 28 August 2022. Online version https://www.thewealthadvisor.com/article/jeremy-siegel-says-its-ok-gamble-speculative-stocks

Chapter One: Forget About Conventional Analysis

1. Joel M. Stern. "Earnings per Share Don't Count." *Financial Analysts Journal* (July–August 1974): 39–43, 67–75.

2. Hans Wagner. "Free Cash Flow Yield: The Best Fundamental Indicator." Investopedia. Updated 2 July 2022. Online version https://www.investopedia.com/articles/fundamental-analysis/09/free-cash-flow-yield.asp

3. Stern. "Earnings per Share Don't Count," 75.

4. Lisa M. Sedor. "An Explanation for Unintentional Optimism in Analysts' Earnings Forecasts." *The Accounting Review* 77, no. 4 (October 2022): 731–753.

5. Sebastian Gell. *Determinants of Earnings Forecast Error, Earnings Forecast Revision and Earnings Forecast Accuracy.* Wiesbaden: Gabler Verlag 2012 and Springer Link.

6. Kenneth S. Lorek and Donald P. Pagash. "Analysts Versus Time-Series Forecasts of Quarterly Earnings: A Maintenance Hypothesis Revisited." *SSRN Electronic Journal* (2014).

7. Tim Koller, Rishi Raj, and Abhishek Saxena. "Avoiding the Consensus-Earnings Trap." *McKinsey & Company.* 2013. Online version https://www.mckinsey.com/~/media/McKinsey/Business%20Functions/Strategy%20and%20Corporate%20Finance/Our%20Insights/Avoiding%20the%20consensus%20earnings%20trap/Avoiding%20the%20consensus%20earnings%20trap.pdf

8. Joshua Livnat and Christine E.L. Tan. "Restatements of Quarterly Earnings: Evidence on Earnings Quality and Market Reactions to the Originally Reported Earnings." New York University Stern School of Business. 2004. Online version https://pages.stern.nyu.edu/~jlivnat/Restatements.pdf

9. Bennett Stewart. *Best Practice EVA: The Definitive Guide to Measuring and Maximizing Shareholder Value.* Hoboken, NJ: John Wiley & Sons, 2013.

10. Peter M. Garber. "Tulipmania." *Journal of Political Economy* 97, no. 3 (June 1989): 535–560.

11. Omaima A.G. Hassan and Frank S. Skinner. "Analyst Coverage: Does the Listing Location Really Matter?" *International Review of Financial Analysis* (July 2016): 227–236. Online version http://bura .brunel.ac.uk/handle/2438/12661

12. "Halfway Through Earnings Season, 80% of S&P 500 Companies Are Beating Estimates." *Barron's*. 5 February 2021. Online version.

13. Ling Cen, Jing Chen, Sudipto Dasgupta, and Vanitha Ragunathan. "Do Analysts and Their Employers Value Access to Management? Evidence from Earnings Conference Call Participation." *Journal of Financial and Quantitative Analysis* (May 2021): 745–787. Online version https://EconPapers.repec.org/ RePEc:cup:jfinqa:v:56:y:2021:i:3:p:745-787_1

14. Lauren Cohen, Dong Lou, and Christopher J. Malloy. "Casting Conference Calls." *Management Science Articles in Advance*. (24 April 2020):2–25. Online version https://pubsonline.informs.org/ doi/10.1287/mnsc.2019.3423

15. Jason Zweig. "Great Groveling, Guys: Counting All the Ways Analysts Fawn over Management." *Wall Street Journal*. 3 March 2017. https://jasonzweig.com/great-groveling-guys-counting-all-the-ways-analysts-fawn-over-management

16. Jonathan A. Milian and Antoinette Smith. "An Investigation of Management During Earnings Conference Calls." *Journal of Behavioral Finance* (8 February 2017): 65–77.

17. Marc Rubinstein. "Great Quarter, Guys." Net Interest. 21 January 2022. https://www.netinterest.co/p/great-quarter-guys

18. Jeff Sommer. "Why You Should Be Wary of Wall Street's Upbeat Stock Forecasts." *New York Times*. 22 July 2022. Online version.

19. Persi Diaconis, Susan Holmes, and Richard Montgomery. "Dynamical Bias in the Coin Toss." *SIAM Review* 1 (2007): 211–235. Online version https://statweb.stanford.edu/~cgates/PERSI/papers/dyn_coin_07.pdf

20. *Godfather: Part II*. 1974. Online version https://www.quotes.net/mquote/37388

21. Fred Imbert. "Warren Buffett Likes Quarterly Earnings Reports from Companies but Not Guidance." CNBC. 30 August 2018. https://www.cnbc.com/2018/08/30/warren-buffett-i-like-quarterly-reports-from-companies-but-not-guidance.html

22. Andrew Lo and Jasmina Hasanhodzic. *Broken Genius: The Heretics of Finance: Conversations with Leading Practitioners of Technical Analysis*. New York: Bloomberg Press, 2009.

Chapter Two: These Are Their Stories

1. Mathias Döpfner. "Elon Musk Reveals Tesla's Plan to Be at the Forefront of a Self-Driving Car Revolution—And Why He Wants to Be Buried on Mars." *Business Insider*. 5 December 2020. https://businessinsider.mx/elon-musk-reveals-teslas-plan-to-be-at-the-forefront-of-a-self-driving-car-revolution-and-why-he-wants-to-be-buried-on-mars/

2. Talon Custer and Vincent G. Piazza. "Devon Energy: Company Outlook." *Bloomberg Intelligence*. 2 January 2020.

Chapter Four: Tip-Offs to Top Stocks

1. Robert W. Holthausen and Richard W. Leftwich. "The Effect of Bond Rating Changes on Common Stock Prices." *Journal of Financial Economics* 17, no. 3 (March 1986): 57–89.

2. Martin S. Fridson and Fernando Alvarez. *Financial Statement Analysis: A Practitioner's Guide*. 5th ed. Hoboken, NJ: John Wiley & Sons, 2022, 328–334.

Glossary

———— ∽ ————

active manager   An asset manager that attempts to produce a higher return than a relevant market index. In contrast, an index fund (SEE) is designed to track an index.

activist investor   An investor or investment management firm that specializes in buying significant minority stakes in public companies with the objective of changing how they're run in order to cause their stock prices to rise. Changes that the activist investor seeks to bring about may include strategic redirection or divestitures.

Amazon Effect   Disruption of traditional brick-and-mortar retailing by eCommerce, the biggest player in which is Amazon.

beat   A corporate release on earnings or another financial performance measure that exceeds analysts' consensus forecast.

big bath   An accounting tactic that makes a bad quarter look even worse, on the theory that a really large loss won't hurt the stock price more than a run-of-the-mill large loss. Taking a big bath can get future write-offs out of the way, enabling the company to report higher earnings in those periods than it otherwise would. A big bath can also create a cookie jar (SEE) for future earnings manipulation.

blockchain   A system, used by cryptocurrencies, to record transactions within a network of linked computers.

blue chip   A stock of a large and well-established company with a reputation for sound finances. Shares of such companies are commonly viewed as comparatively safe investments.

central processing unit (CPU)   The electronic circuitry that executes the instructions making up a computer program. It's distinct from specialized processors such as graphics processing units (SEE).

CEO   The acronym for Chief Executive Officer, who is usually the corporation's top manager.

channel-stuffing   Shipping more goods to distributors or wholesalers than they can normally sell within the coming period. A company engaged in the practice can book sales on the extra merchandise shipped, thereby inflating its current earnings.

chartist   A trader or analyst who relies on technical analysis (SEE).

conglomerate   A corporation that operates in several widely divergent businesses. This corporate form was popular in the 1960s but has become less common over time.

cookie jar   An accounting reserve that can be dipped into for the purpose of reporting a steady rise in earnings. The reserve may contain artificially created losses that can subsequently be reversed and liabilities that can be canceled to produce reportable income.

CPU   See **central processing unit**.

cryptocurrency   A digital or virtual currency, usually not controlled by a government. Many cryptocurrencies utilize **blockchain** (SEE) technology.

crypto-miner   A person or firm engaged in the process that puts new units of a cryptocurrency (SEE) into circulation. The crypto-miner attempts to solve a complex math problem in hopes of obtaining the next cryptocurrency units to be issued.

depreciation   An accounting entry on the income statement meant to represent a tangible asset's loss of value over time through wear and tear.

dispersion   A measure of the extent to which numbers, such as analysts' price targets (SEE) are spread out. See also **Fridson-Lee statistic**.

earnings management   The practice of artificially inflating reported earnings by taking advantage of the discretion afforded to management in certain accounting decisions.

earnings per share (EPS)   A financial ratio widely used in stock valuation. It is calculated as net income divided by the number of common shares outstanding.

EBITDA   The acronym for the profitability measure composed of earnings before interest, taxes, depreciation (SEE), and amortization.

economic profit   The true amount of profit generated by a company, taking into account all explicit and implicit costs. This contrasts with GAAP (SEE) earnings, which are calculated partly on the basis of discretionary accounting decisions.

economic value added (EVA)   A profit measure based on the principles that (a) genuine profitability results when value is created for shareholders and (b) projects should earn returns that exceed their cost of capital. It is calculated as net operating profit after tax minus (weighted average cost of capital times capital invested). Capital invested is the sum of equity and long-term debt at the beginning of the period.

efficient markets   The notion that superior risk-adjusted returns are unachievable because the market instantly arbitrages away any mispricing that temporarily arises. Adherents of this view generally invest in index funds (SEE).

electric vehicle (EV)   A vehicle propelled by one or more electric motors. Modern versions of these vehicles are displacing gasoline-powered vehicles utilizing internal combustion engines.

EPS   See **earnings per share**.

EV   See **electric vehicle**.

EVA   See **economic value added**.

fallen angel   A corporate bond that was rated investment-grade (SEE) at the time of issue but was subsequently downgraded to speculative-grade (SEE).

FASB   See **Financial Accounting Standards Board**.

Federal Reserve   The central bank of the United States. Through its Federal Open Market Committee the Federal Reserve manages interest rate policy with the dual objectives of limiting inflation and holding down the level of unemployment.

Financial Accounting Standards Board (FASB)   An independent, nonprofit organization with authority recognized by the Securities and Exchange Commission to establish U.S. accounting and financial reporting standards for companies and nonprofit organizations.

free cash flow   A financial performance measure defined as cash flow from operations less capital expenditures.

Fridson-Lee statistic   A measure of dispersion (SEE) in analysts' EPS (SEE) estimates for a stock. It is calculated as the highest estimate minus the lowest estimate, divided by the lowest estimate.

fundamental analysis   Determination of a stock's intrinsic value by examination of pertinent economic and financial factors, including, but not limited to, prevailing economic and industry conditions, the company's financial strength, and quality of management.

GAAP   See **Generally Accepted Accounting Principles**

Generally Accepted Accounting Principles (GAAP)   The set of accounting rules that U.S. public companies are required to use for financial reporting.

goodwill   An intangible asset created on a company's balance sheet when it acquires another company for more than the fair value of its net assets. Goodwill is meant to represent the value of intangible factors such as the acquired company's brands, customer relationships, and proprietary technology.

GPU   See **graphics processing unit**.

graphics processing unit (GPU)   A chip or electronic circuit that enables graphics to be displayed on an electronic device. GPUs are used in videogames and by crypto-miners (SEE).

gross margin   A profitability measure that is calculated as net sales minus cost of goods sold.

guidance   An informal report by a company that indicates management's expectation for future EPS (SEE) or other performance measure.

high-yield bond   A corporate bond that is rated speculative-grade (SEE) but not in default.

indenture A contract between bondholders and a corporate bond issuer that spells out such items as maturity date, interest rate, provisions for redemption prior to maturity, and events of default.

independent power producer A non-utility company that owns power-generation facilities and sells electricity to utilities and end users.

index fund A passively managed mutual fund or exchange-traded fund that follows predetermined rules in order to track a chosen basket of underlying investments.

INSEAD A contraction of "Institut Européen d'Administration des Affaires," a business school headquartered in Fontainebleau, France, with campuses in Europe, Asia, the Middle East, and North America.

inverter In the field of solar power, a device that converts the direct current (DC) output of a solar panel into the alternating current (AC) used by the grid and off-grid networks.

investment-grade A corporate bond rating in the range of Aaa to Baa3 (Moody's) or AAA to BBB– (Standard & Poor's and Fitch Ratings).

junk bond A derogatory term for a high-yield bond (SEE).

leverage (financial) Use of borrowed funds, such as corporate bonds and term loans, along with equity, in a company's capital structure. Leverage increases a company's return on equity (SEE) when its return is positive and reduces it when the return is negative.

miss   A corporate release on earnings or another financial performance measure that falls short of analysts' consensus forecast.

MLPE   See **module-level power electronics**.

module-level power electronics (MLPE)   Devices that can be incorporated into solar photovoltaic (SEE) systems to provide benefits that include improved performance where shade is present.

nanometer   One-billionth of a meter. The diameter of a pinhead measures approximately one million nanometers.

New Economy   A term that refers to high-growth, leading-edge technology industries that started to become much more prominent in the U.S. economy in the late 1990s. This marked a transition from the economy's earlier concentration in manufacturing and commodities.

New York Mercantile Exchange   A commodity futures exchange owned and operated by CME Group. Energy carriers, metals, and other commodities are traded on the exchange.

optimizer   A direct current (DC) to alternating current (AC) converter technology that maximizes the energy produced by solar photovoltaic (SEE) or wind turbine systems.

outlook (bond rating) An opinion by a rating agency regarding the likely direction of a company's rating over the medium term. An outlook may be Positive, Stable, Negative, or Developing.

PE multiple A valuation measure defined as share price divided by earnings per share (SEE). The multiple can be calculated on either trailing or projected earnings.

Philadelphia Stock Exchange Semiconductor Index A capitalization-weighted index composed of the 30 largest U.S. companies that are primarily involved with semiconductor design, manufacturing, distribution, and sales.

photovoltaics Conversion of light into electricity using semiconducting materials.

point-and-figure chart A technical analysis (SEE) tool that plots price movements without considering the passage of time.

price target The share price at which an analyst considers a stock fairly valued, based on its projected and historical earnings.

quant A practitioner of quantitative investing, which employs sophisticated mathematical modeling, and data analysis to gauge the probability of profiting on a trade.

renewable energy Energy obtained from resources that naturally replenish themselves on a human timescale.

Examples include sunlight, wind, water currents and tides, and geothermal heat.

return on equity (ROE) A financial performance measure calculated as net income divided by shareholders' equity. The denominator may be defined as the average of beginning and ending shareholders' equity for the period.

rising star A corporate bond that was rated speculative-grade (SEE) at the time of issue but was subsequently upgraded to investment-grade (SEE).

ROE See **return on equity**.

S&P 500 Formally the Standard & Poor's 500. A float-weighted/capitalization-weighted index of large stocks listed on U.S. exchanges.

Sarbanes-Oxley Act A law enacted by Congress in 2002 with the aim of protecting investors from fraudulent financial reporting. The legislation's passage followed a series of major accounting scandals.

senior secured A type of debt that stands first in line for payment, in the event that the borrower becomes financially distressed. This debt is backed by assets that are pledged as collateral.

short-covering The process by which a **short seller** (SEE) closes out a position by purchasing shares to replace the shares borrowed in opening the position. Short-covering in a stock that has risen, confounding short sellers' expectations, can propel the stock even higher.

short seller   A market participant who bets that a stock will decline in price. The short seller sells the stock, delivering borrowed shares. If the trade is successful, the short seller will buy the stock at a lower price, thereby netting a profit, and return shares to the stock lender.

SPAC   See **special purpose acquisition**.

special dividend   A nonrecurring dividend paid in addition to a company's regular dividend. It may occur in connection with an event such as a realignment of operations.

special purpose acquisition (SPAC)   A company formed to raise capital through an initial public offering to be used to acquire an operating business.

speculative-grade   A corporate bond rating in the range of Ba1 to C (Moody's) or BB+ to D (Standard & Poor's and Fitch Ratings).

standard deviation   A statistical measure that is used to quantify volatility (SEE) of stock returns or prices.

subcertification   A process by which a CEO (SEE) can fulfill the **Sarbanes-Oxley Act** (SEE) requirement of certifying the company's financial statements, yet potentially avoid liability for misstatements by making that certification subject to the accuracy of certification performed by subordinates.

subordinated   A type of debt that ranks below senior debt in priority of payment, in the event that the borrower becomes financially distressed.

technical analysis   A form of securities analysis that aims to predict future price movements based on past market data, including price changes and volume.

total return   a measure of return that takes into account price appreciation, dividends, and reinvestment of dividends

trading rule   A plan to execute a trade when certain conditions arise, based on a belief in the potential for profiting from certain recurring patterns in price movements.

tulip mania   A large run-up in the Dutch market for tulip bulbs that culminated in a crash in 1637. Euphoric periods in stock market cycles are commonly likened to tulip mania, but the actual history and lessons of tulip mania are matters of controversy among financial historians and theoreticians.

volatility   A measure of the dispersion (SEE) of returns of a stock or an index. Highly volatile stocks are generally considered high-risk investments. In fact, a major strain of financial theory essentially equates volatility with risk.

West Texas Intermediate (WTI)   A light, sweet grade of crude oil that is one of the most prominent benchmarks for oil prices.

WTI   See **West Texas Intermediate**.

zero-pollution emission air pollution credit   A payment made to generators of electricity for not emitting greenhouse gases process. Electric vehicles (SEE) can qualify for the credit.

About the Author

MARTIN FRIDSON IS CHIEF INVESTMENT OFFICER at Lehmann Livian Fridson Advisors. He has received the CFA Society New York's Ben Graham Award and was named the Financial Management Association International's Financial Executive of the Year. Fridson has served as a consultant to the Federal Reserve Board of Governors and as Special Assistant to the Director for Deferred Compensation, Office of Management and the Budget, The City of New York. He is a graduate of Harvard College and Harvard Business School.

Index

~

Page numbers followed by *t* indicate tables, charts, or graphs.